Navigating Bipolar Disorder

Empowering Patients and Families with Knowledge, Strategies, and Hope in the Journey Through Bipolar Disorder Management and Care

Karina Gibson

Table of Contents

Introduction

As a seasoned psychiatrist, my professional journey has been deeply intertwined with the lives of individuals battling bipolar disorder. This experience has not only enriched my understanding of the disorder but also highlighted the resilience and strength of those affected and their families. "Navigating Bipolar Disorder" is a distillation of years of clinical practice, research, and heartfelt conversations, crafted to empower both individuals grappling with this condition and their loved ones. This book is conceived as a beacon of hope, illuminating the path through the complexities of bipolar disorder with clarity, empathy, and insight.

Bipolar disorder, characterized by significant mood swings that can range from the highs of mania to the depths of depression, poses unique challenges. It affects every aspect of an individual's life, influencing their thoughts, feelings, behaviors, and relationships. The journey to understand and manage bipolar disorder can often feel overwhelming, and fraught with uncertainties and challenges. It is here that "Navigating Bipolar Disorder" seeks to make a difference, offering a comprehensive guide that bridges the gap between medical knowledge and the lived experiences of those affected.

The book starts by laying down a strong groundwork for comprehension. It meticulously dissects bipolar disorder, clarifying its definition and explaining the distinctions between its various types, including Bipolar I, Bipolar II, and Cyclothymia. This section aims to equip readers with the essential knowledge to navigate the disorder, debunking myths and misconceptions that surround it. By demystifying the condition, the book fosters an environment of knowledge and understanding, crucial for reducing stigma and promoting empathy.

An essential component of managing bipolar disorder is the support network surrounding the individual. "Navigating Bipolar Disorder" delves into the transformative power of a well-informed and empathetic support system. It explores the multifaceted roles that loved ones can assume, from confidantes and supporters to advocates and caregivers. This guidance is designed to highlight how each role contributes significantly to the well-being of individuals with bipolar disorder, offering practical advice on how to provide effective support. This includes navigating the complexities of emotional support and practical assistance, all while maintaining a delicate balance between offering help and respecting the individual's autonomy.

Empowerment is at the heart of this guide. The book champions the idea that individuals with bipolar disorder, armed with the right strategies and knowledge, can lead fulfilling lives. It encourages readers to take an active role in their treatment and management, advocating for a personalized approach that considers the unique circumstances of each individual. This empowerment extends to families and friends, equipping them with the tools to provide meaningful support and advocate for their loved one's needs.

Moreover, "Navigating Bipolar Disorder" serves as a call to action for greater advocacy and awareness. It underscores the importance of fostering a deeper societal understanding of bipolar disorder, challenging stigma, and advocating for improved mental health services. By sharing personal stories and insights, the book aims to inspire readers to become advocates for change, contributing to a more inclusive and compassionate society.

Writing this book, I envisioned creating a resource that transcends the traditional patient-doctor dynamic. I aimed to offer a guide that feels like a conversation, a shared journey towards understanding and empowerment. This book is intended for anyone touched by bipolar disorder—whether personally experiencing the condition, supporting a loved one, or simply seeking to understand more about this complex mental health challenge.

In "Navigating Bipolar Disorder," readers will find not only a compilation of medical facts and treatment strategies but also a source of comfort and hope. It is a testament to the power of knowledge, empathy, and community in the face of mental health challenges. Through its pages, I invite readers to embark on a journey of discovery, learning, and growth. Together, we can navigate the complexities of bipolar disorder, armed with the insights and strategies needed to thrive.

CHAPTER 1

Understanding Bipolar Disorder

This chapter serves as your foundational guide to unraveling the complexities of a condition often shrouded in misconception. We begin by defining bipolar disorder, illuminating the various types and symptoms that mark this mental health condition. Our exploration extends to the underlying causes—genetic, environmental, and neurobiological factors—that interplay to influence its development.

Moving beyond mere definitions, we confront and dispel the myths that cloud the public perception of bipolar disorder, providing a clearer, more accurate picture. The journey continues as we outline the diagnostic process, offering insight into what individuals can expect as they seek understanding and management strategies.

Defining Bipolar Disorder: Types and Symptoms

Bipolar disorder stands as a significant challenge within the realm of mental health, characterized by its diverse manifestations and the profound impact it has on those it affects. This condition, once broadly categorized under the term 'manic depression,' has evolved in our understanding into a nuanced spectrum of disorders, each with unique diagnostic criteria, symptoms, and treatment approaches. Our exploration here aims to dissect these complexities, offering an in-depth look at the various classifications of bipolar disorder and the distinct symptoms that define each, thereby providing a foundational knowledge base for both individuals experiencing these conditions and their support networks.

Bipolar I Disorder is marked by the occurrence of one or more manic episodes. These episodes are identifiable as specific durations marked by abnormally prolonged periods of heightened, expansive, or irritable mood, accompanied by sustained increases in activity or energy, lasting a minimum of seven days, or shorter if hospitalization is necessary. The manic episodes may be preceded or followed by hypomanic or major depressive episodes, but it is the presence of the manic episode that defines this subtype. Symptoms of mania comprise heightened self-esteem or grandiosity, reduced need for sleep, increased verbosity or a compulsion to keep speaking, rapid flow of thoughts or a perception of racing thoughts, distractibility, heightened pursuit of goals, physical restlessness, and excessive engagement in activities carrying significant risks.

Bipolar II Disorder, while sharing some similarities with Bipolar I, is specifically characterized by a pattern of one or more major depressive episodes accompanied by at least one hypomanic episode. Unlike the full-blown manic episodes seen in Bipolar I, hypomanic episodes are less severe and do not result in the significant functional impairment typical of manic episodes. However, the depressive episodes that occur in Bipolar II can be just as severe and debilitating as those in Bipolar I, making this condition equally serious and worthy of attention and care.

Cyclothymic Disorder or cyclothymia is identified by periods of hypomanic symptoms intermixed with periods of depressive symptoms lasting for at least two years (one year in children and adolescents). Importantly, these symptoms do not meet the full criteria for a hypomanic episode or a major depressive episode during this period. Cyclothymia is marked by chronic, fluctuating mood disturbances, with symptoms not absent for more than two months at a time. This subtype underscores the spectrum nature of bipolar disorder, demonstrating that symptoms can persist over a long duration without necessarily reaching the full threshold of manic or major depressive episodes.

The DSM-5 also acknowledges **other specified and unspecified bipolar and related disorders**, catering to those instances where individuals exhibit significant bipolar symptoms that do not neatly fit the criteria of the aforementioned categories. This includes, for example, short-duration hypomanic episodes (lasting less than four days) or hypomanic episodes without preceding major depressive episodes, highlighting the diversity and individual variability within bipolar spectrum disorders.

Adding further complexity to bipolar disorder's heterogeneity are features such as **rapid cycling** and **mixed features**. Rapid cycling is characterized by four or more mood episodes in a single year and is known to complicate treatment and prognosis. Mixed features refer to the presence of simultaneous symptoms of opposite mood polarities during manic, hypomanic, or depressive episodes, adding a layer of complexity to diagnosis and treatment.

In sum, the spectrum of bipolar disorder encompasses a range of conditions, each with its own set of challenges and requirements for care. Understanding the breadth of this spectrum and the specific characteristics of each classification is crucial for effective treatment and support.

The Causes of Bipolar Disorder

The etiology of bipolar disorder is a tapestry woven from the threads of genetic predisposition, environmental stressors, and neurobiological alterations, creating a complex picture that defies simplistic explanations. This multifaceted nature underscores the importance of a nuanced understanding of the disorder, one that embraces its complexity and advocates for a destigmatized perspective. Here, we delve into the depths of these contributing factors, exploring how each plays a pivotal role in the development of bipolar disorder and how their interplay might inform our approach to treatment and support.

Genetic Predisposition

Research has consistently underscored the significance of genetics in the risk of developing bipolar disorder. Family, twin, and adoption studies reveal a higher prevalence of the disorder among first-degree relatives of individuals with bipolar disorder, suggesting a heritable component. The heritability estimates for bipolar disorder are among the highest for psychiatric disorders, with studies indicating that genetics account for approximately 60-80% of the risk.

However, the genetic architecture of bipolar disorder is complex, involving multiple genes each contributing a small effect rather than a single causative gene. Recent genome-wide association studies (GWAS) have identified several genetic markers associated with an increased risk of bipolar disorder, although these markers collectively explain only a small fraction of the genetic risk, pointing to the involvement of numerous genes and the potential influence of gene-environment interactions.

Environmental Stressors

The impact of environmental factors on the development of bipolar disorder is an area of intense research and interest. Stressful life events, trauma, and socio-cultural factors have been identified as significant contributors to the onset and progression of the disorder. Individuals with bipolar disorder often report a higher incidence of stressful life events before the onset of the disorder, suggesting that these events smay trigger the manifestation of symptoms in genetically predisposed individuals.

Moreover, the nature of these stressors can vary widely, from childhood adversity and trauma to major life changes or chronic stress, underscoring the diverse ways in which environmental factors can impact an individual's vulnerability to bipolar disorder.

Neurobiological Changes

Advancements in neuroimaging techniques have shed light on the structural and functional brain differences in individuals with bipolar disorder, offering insights into the neurobiological underpinnings of the disorder. Structural MRI studies have identified alterations in brain areas involved in emotion regulation, such as the prefrontal cortex, amygdala, and hippocampus, in individuals with bipolar disorder. These changes may contribute to the emotional dysregulation characteristic of the disorder.

Functional MRI (fMRI) studies have further elucidated abnormalities in the neural circuits connecting these regions, suggesting disruptions in the networks responsible for mood regulation. Additionally, neurochemical studies have pointed to imbalances in neurotransmitter systems, including dopamine, serotonin, and glutamate, which play critical roles in mood stabilization.

The interaction between genetic predisposition, environmental stressors, and neurobiological changes is key to understanding the development of bipolar disorder. Genetic factors may confer a baseline vulnerability to the disorder, which can be triggered or exacerbated by environmental stressors. These stressors, in turn, may induce neurobiological changes that manifest as the symptoms of bipolar disorder. This model emphasizes the importance of considering the disorder within the context of an individual's unique genetic makeup and life experiences.

In dissecting the complexity of these contributing factors, it is crucial to move beyond reductionist views of bipolar disorder as solely a genetic or environmental condition. The interplay of genetics, environment, and neurobiology highlights the multifactorial nature of the disorder and underscores the need for a comprehensive approach to treatment that addresses not only the biological aspects but also the psychological and social dimensions. Current research continues to explore these relationships, aiming to unravel the intricate mechanisms that underlie bipolar disorder and to pave the way for more effective, personalized interventions.

By embracing the complexity of bipolar disorder's etiology, we can foster a deeper understanding of the condition, one that recognizes the diverse pathways to its development and the varied experiences of those affected. This understanding is crucial for destigmatizing bipolar disorder, promoting empathy, and advancing our efforts to provide meaningful support and treatment to individuals and their families navigating the challenges of this condition.

Debunking Myths

Bipolar disorder is often shrouded in misconception and stigma, leading to widespread misunderstanding about its nature and impact on those affected. By confronting and debunking these pervasive myths with empirical evidence and expert consensus, we aim to foster a culture of understanding and acceptance, challenging stereotypes that hinder societal integration and self-acceptance of individuals with bipolar disorder.

Myth 1: Bipolar Disorder Is Just Extreme Moodiness

One of the most pervasive myths about bipolar disorder is that it's synonymous with simple moodiness or emotional instability that everyone experiences from time to time. This misunderstanding minimizes the seriousness of bipolar disorder, which is a clinical condition involving significant mood episodes that are distinct in their severity, duration, and impact on daily functioning. Unlike ordinary mood fluctuations, manic episodes in bipolar disorder can lead to drastic changes in behavior and judgment, resulting in serious consequences, such as financial loss, relationship breakdowns, or the need for hospitalization.

Depressive episodes, on the other hand, are characterized by intense feelings of sadness, hopelessness, and an inability to experience pleasure, often leading to significant impairment in personal, social, and occupational domains. The diagnostic criteria for bipolar disorder, as outlined in the DSM-5, require these mood episodes to last a specific duration (at least a week for mania, four days for hypomania, and two weeks for depression) and to be accompanied by a distinct set of symptoms, underscoring the clinical nature of the condition.

Myth 2: Bipolar Disorder Signifies a Weak Character or Unreliability

The stigmatization of bipolar disorder as a character flaw or a marker of unreliability is not only harmful but also unfounded. This stereotype perpetuates a misunderstanding of bipolar disorder as a moral failing rather than a medical condition. It's critical to understand that bipolar disorder is rooted in complex biological and environmental factors, including genetic predisposition and neurobiological changes, and is not a reflection of an individual's character or strength.

The portrayal of individuals with bipolar disorder as inherently unreliable neglects the reality that, with appropriate treatment and support, many manage their condition effectively and lead successful, fulfilling lives. This myth also discourages individuals from seeking the help they need, fearing judgment or discrimination, further isolating those affected.

Myth 3: Individuals with Bipolar Disorder Cannot Lead Stable, Productive Lives

Contrary to the misconception that individuals with bipolar disorder are incapable of leading stable, productive lives, many people with the condition achieve remarkable success in various fields. This myth fails to account for the efficacy of current treatment modalities, which can significantly mitigate the symptoms of bipolar disorder and enhance an individual's ability to function. Comprehensive treatment plans, tailored to the individual's needs, often include medication, psychotherapy, and lifestyle adjustments.

With these interventions, along with supportive relationships and accommodations, individuals with bipolar disorder can and do lead fulfilling lives. Highlighting the achievements of those with bipolar disorder challenges this stereotype and emphasizes the potential for resilience and accomplishment.

Myth 4: Treatment for Bipolar Disorder Is Ineffective

The notion that treatment for bipolar disorder is ineffective is a dangerous myth that can deter individuals from seeking necessary care. Advances in psychiatric medication, psychotherapeutic techniques, and holistic care approaches have significantly improved the outlook for individuals with bipolar disorder. While it's true that treatment is highly individualized and may require adjustments to find the most effective regimen, the potential for treatment to improve quality of life is undeniable.

Medications like mood stabilizers, antipsychotics, and antidepressants, in combination with psychotherapy methods such as cognitive-behavioral therapy (CBT) and family-focused therapy, have proven beneficial for many. Additionally, lifestyle interventions, including regular exercise, sleep hygiene, and stress management, play a crucial role in managing the condition. The effectiveness of treatment is supported by a wealth of clinical research and the lived experiences of individuals with bipolar disorder, underscoring the importance of debunking this myth to encourage those affected to pursue and maintain treatment.

By addressing these myths head-on, we challenge the misinformation and stereotypes that have long surrounded bipolar disorder. Our goal is to replace misconceptions with a nuanced understanding grounded in scientific evidence and clinical expertise. In doing so, we advocate for a more informed, empathetic approach to bipolar disorder that recognizes the dignity and potential of every individual affected by the condition.

Diagnosing Bipolar Disorder

Diagnosing bipolar disorder is a meticulous process that demands precision and patience, aiming to ensure that individuals receive accurate assessments and appropriate care pathways. This journey often begins when individuals, notice significant mood disturbances in their lives and seek professional help. The diagnostic process is multifaceted, involving a series of steps designed to differentiate bipolar disorder from other mental health conditions with overlapping symptoms.

Initial Consultation

The initial consultation for diagnosing bipolar disorder is a critical juncture where healthcare professionals embark on a comprehensive exploration of the patient's mental health history, current symptoms, and the overall impact these have on daily functioning. This step is instrumental in establishing a rapport and trust between the patient and clinician, setting a foundation for open communication. It involves a detailed discussion about past psychiatric history, any treatments received, and a thorough review of symptoms indicative of manic, hypomanic, or depressive episodes.

The objective is to gather a nuanced understanding of the patient's experiences, their health history, and how their symptoms influence their life, aiming to guide the diagnostic and treatment planning process effectively. Moreover, the initial consultation is an opportunity to set expectations for the diagnostic journey ahead, outlining the steps, potential further assessments, and the collaborative nature of developing a treatment plan. It's a pivotal moment that emphasizes empathy, patient-centered care, and the importance of a tailored approach to managing bipolar disorder.

By focusing on understanding the individual's unique experiences and how bipolar disorder impacts their life, healthcare professionals can foster a therapeutic relationship built on trust, thereby facilitating a more accurate diagnosis and establishing the groundwork for effective treatment.

Diagnostic Interviews

Diagnostic interviews are a pivotal element in the assessment and diagnosis of bipolar disorder, offering a structured opportunity for healthcare professionals to delve into an individual's psychiatric history and present symptoms in depth. Utilizing criteria primarily from the Diagnostic and Statistical Manual of Mental Disorders (DSM-5), these interviews meticulously evaluate the occurrence, duration, and intensity of manic, hypomanic, and depressive episodes.

By investigating the nature of these mood episodes, including any accompanying behaviors and thought patterns, clinicians can distinguish bipolar disorder from other mental health conditions, ensuring an accurate diagnosis. This process not only aids in understanding the specific manifestations of the disorder in the individual but also plays a crucial role in differential diagnosis, helping to identify the most appropriate and effective treatment approach.

Throughout the diagnostic interview, the emphasis is placed on creating an environment of trust and openness, encouraging patients to share their experiences without reservation. This collaborative approach is essential for capturing the full spectrum of the disorder's impact on the individual's life, facilitating a diagnosis that truly reflects their unique situation.

Patients can expect to engage in a detailed discussion of their mental health history, symptomatology, and the effect of these on their daily functioning. The outcome of this interview will guide the subsequent steps in the diagnostic journey, potentially including further assessments or interventions, with the ultimate goal of crafting a tailored treatment plan that addresses the individual's specific needs and challenges.

Psychological Questionnaires

Psychological questionnaires are an integral component of the diagnostic process for bipolar disorder, serving as standardized tools to assess the range and severity of symptoms experienced by the individual. These instruments, such as the Mood Disorder Questionnaire (MDQ) for manic or hypomanic episodes and the Beck Depression Inventory (BDI) for depressive symptoms, offer a structured approach to gathering vital information.

By quantifying symptoms over a specific timeframe, these questionnaires provide clinicians with detailed insights into the patient's mental health status, highlighting patterns of mood swings and behaviors indicative of bipolar disorder. The systematic nature of these assessments ensures a comprehensive evaluation of symptoms, facilitating an accurate diagnosis when used in conjunction with detailed clinical interviews.

The process of completing these questionnaires typically involves the individual responding to a series of statements that reflect common symptoms and behaviors associated with bipolar disorder, with responses indicating the frequency and intensity of these experiences. The interpretation of questionnaire results is a collaborative effort, integrating the clinician's expertise and the patient's personal experiences. This approach underscores the importance of a patient-centered diagnostic process, allowing for a nuanced understanding of the individual's condition.

By incorporating psychological questionnaires into the assessment for bipolar disorder, healthcare professionals are better equipped to distinguish between bipolar disorder and other mental health conditions, guiding the creation of a customized treatment strategy that meets the specific requirements of the individual.

Differential Diagnosis

Differential diagnosis is a pivotal step in diagnosing bipolar disorder, distinguishing it from other mental health conditions with overlapping symptoms. This meticulous process involves evaluating the individual's symptoms against the criteria for various disorders, such as unipolar depression, ADHD, and anxiety disorders, using diagnostic criteria from sources like the DSM-5.

Healthcare professionals utilize a range of tools, including detailed psychological evaluations and additional questionnaires, to systematically rule out other conditions. This phase is crucial for ensuring the diagnosis accurately reflects the individual's condition, as the treatment strategies for bipolar disorder significantly differ from those for other mental health issues, particularly in the use of medications and psychotherapeutic approaches. The collaborative and multidisciplinary nature of differential diagnosis means that psychiatrists, psychologists, and possibly other specialists work together to achieve a comprehensive understanding of the patient's mental health.

Individuals undergoing this process can expect to engage in a series of assessments, providing detailed personal and family histories to aid in distinguishing bipolar disorder from similar conditions. This step is vital not only for establishing an accurate diagnosis but also for informing a tailored treatment plan that addresses the specific needs of the individual, ensuring the best possible outcomes in managing bipolar disorder.

Neuroimaging and Other Assessments

Neuroimaging and other specialized assessments can play a significant role in the diagnostic process for bipolar disorder, particularly in complex cases where differential diagnosis is challenging or when co-occurring neurological conditions are suspected. Techniques like Magnetic Resonance Imaging (MRI) and Computed Tomography (CT) scans are utilized to explore structural brain abnormalities, while functional MRI (fMRI) and Positron Emission Tomography (PET) scans assess brain activity, shedding light on the functional anomalies that may be associated with bipolar disorder.

These imaging tools, complemented by blood tests for metabolic or hormonal imbalances and, less commonly, Electroencephalogram (EEG) tests for seizure disorders, provide a comprehensive overview of an individual's neurobiological status, aiding in the accurate diagnosis of bipolar disorder and the exclusion of other medical conditions that might present with similar symptoms. For individuals undergoing these assessments, the process typically involves referral to specialists or medical facilities equipped with the necessary technology, with procedures that are non-invasive and generally considered safe.

Patients can expect clear guidance on preparation and what to anticipate during the scanning process, which is designed to be as comfortable as possible. While neuroimaging findings alone do not constitute a diagnosis of bipolar disorder, they are invaluable in contributing to a holistic understanding of the individual's condition, ensuring that the diagnosis is accurate and that any co-occurring issues are appropriately addressed. This integrative approach, combining clinical evaluation with advanced diagnostic tools, underscores the commitment to providing personalized, evidence-based care for individuals with bipolar disorder.

The Collaborative Aspect of Diagnosis

The diagnosis of bipolar disorder transcends the traditional boundaries of a unidirectional assessment, embodying a collaborative approach that engages not only the patient but also their family and a multidisciplinary team of healthcare professionals. This collaborative aspect is pivotal, recognizing that the insights and experiences of those closest to the patient can significantly enrich the understanding of the individual's condition.

Family members can offer invaluable observations about the patient's behavior, mood changes, and the effects these have on their daily lives, which might not always be apparent or fully disclosed by the patient themselves. Moreover, the involvement of various specialists, including psychiatrists, psychologists, and possibly neurologists or other healthcare providers, ensures a comprehensive evaluation from multiple perspectives. This multidisciplinary approach facilitates a more accurate diagnosis by integrating diverse expertise, allowing for a holistic view of the patient's mental health.

Within this collaborative framework, the patient's active participation is crucial. They are encouraged to share their experiences, concerns, and expectations openly, contributing to a deeper mutual understanding and a more personalized diagnostic process. This engagement is essential for constructing an accurate portrayal of the patient's mental health, fostering a sense of agency and involvement in their journey toward diagnosis and treatment.

By emphasizing the collaborative aspect of diagnosis, the process becomes a shared journey, aiming to demystify the complexities of bipolar disorder and prepare the ground for an effective, tailored treatment plan. This approach not only enhances the accuracy of the diagnosis but also strengthens the therapeutic relationship, setting a positive precedent for the ongoing management of the condition.

Preparing for the Diagnostic Outcome

Preparing for the diagnostic outcomes of bipolar disorder is a critical phase in the journey toward understanding and managing the condition. This stage is about setting realistic expectations and preparing mentally and emotionally for the results that will guide future treatment and management strategies. Patients are encouraged to engage in open dialogues with their healthcare providers about the potential diagnoses and the implications of each outcome.

This preparation involves discussing the nature of bipolar disorder, the possibility of other diagnoses if symptoms overlap with different mental health conditions, and the impact of an accurate diagnosis on treatment options and lifestyle adjustments. Understanding that bipolar disorder is a manageable condition with the right treatment plan is crucial, and healthcare professionals play a key role in providing reassurance and information to mitigate concerns and anxieties about the diagnosis. Moreover, preparing for the diagnostic outcomes also means understanding the comprehensive nature of treatment for bipolar disorder, which may include medication, psychotherapy, lifestyle modifications, and support networks.

Patients are encouraged to think about questions or concerns they might have regarding these treatments, including potential side effects of medications, the commitment required for psychotherapy, and ways to integrate treatment into their daily lives. This preparation ensures that patients are ready to take an active role in their treatment and management of bipolar disorder, fostering a collaborative approach to care.

Healthcare providers may also suggest resources such as support groups, educational materials, and counseling services for both patients and their families to help them navigate the complexities of the condition, emphasizing that a diagnosis is not just a label but a step towards better health and quality of life.

Post-Diagnosis Pathways

After receiving a bipolar disorder diagnosis, individuals embark on a tailored treatment and management journey, crucial for navigating the condition effectively. This phase involves a comprehensive dialogue between the healthcare provider and the patient about the nature of bipolar disorder, potential treatment avenues—including medication, psychotherapy, and lifestyle modifications—and the importance of building a supportive network.

Treatments may encompass mood stabilizers, antipsychotics, and psychoeducational interventions, aimed at equipping patients with coping strategies for symptom management and stress reduction. The plan emphasizes the significance of the patient's active involvement in their care, advocating for an adaptive approach that may evolve to meet changing needs over time. This collaborative, dynamic strategy underlines the transition from diagnosis to a structured, informed pathway toward better health, emphasizing resilience, informed decision-making, and the cultivation of a supportive environment for managing bipolar disorder.

By demystifying the diagnostic process and emphasizing the steps involved in accurately diagnosing bipolar disorder, individuals and their families can be better prepared to navigate this journey. An accurate diagnosis is the cornerstone of effective management, paving the way for tailored treatment plans that address the unique needs of each individual.

Bipolar Disorder in Daily Life

Living with bipolar disorder intertwines intricately with the fabric of daily life, presenting unique challenges and opportunities for growth in personal relationships, professional endeavors, and the journey of self-care. Understanding and managing the ebbs and flows of manic and depressive episodes demand not only a robust support system but also an internal resilience and adaptability from those affected. The essence of navigating life with bipolar disorder lies in setting realistic expectations—acknowledging that while the path may be unpredictable, it is navigable with appropriate strategies and support.

The domain of personal relationships often bears the brunt of bipolar disorder's impact. Manic episodes can lead to impulsive decisions that strain relationships, while depressive phases might result in withdrawal from social interactions, affecting connections with family and friends. Open communication becomes a cornerstone here, facilitating a mutual understanding that can bridge gaps created by mood swings. Crafting an environment where experiences and feelings can be shared openly paves the way for stronger, more understanding relationships that can withstand the challenges posed by the disorder.

In the professional sphere, bipolar disorder introduces complexities that necessitate a nuanced approach to career development and workplace dynamics. The fluctuating nature of the condition can affect job performance, prompting concerns over disclosure and the pursuit of accommodations. Individuals must navigate the delicate balance between seeking necessary support and managing potential stigma, a task that requires courage and strategic planning. Workplace accommodations, flexible scheduling, and understanding from employers and colleagues can significantly enhance occupational success and satisfaction.

Self-care emerges as a pivotal theme in managing bipolar disorder, encompassing not just adherence to medication but also engagement in activities that promote overall well-being. Regular exercise, a nutritious diet, and a consistent sleep schedule form the pillars of a healthy lifestyle that can mitigate the intensity of mood swings. Psychotherapy and counseling offer spaces for reflection and the development of coping strategies, empowering individuals to understand their triggers and responses better. Furthermore, support groups and online forums provide invaluable resources for connection and exchange, offering insights and camaraderie from those on similar journeys.

Setting and managing expectations regarding treatment outcomes is another critical aspect of living with bipolar disorder. The journey towards stabilization is often characterized by trials and adjustments in medication and therapy to find the most effective combination for each individual. It's a path marked by patience, persistence, and the understanding that progress may be gradual. The objective is not a cure but a management of symptoms that allows for a fulfilling life.

Illustrative of the diverse experiences within the bipolar spectrum are the stories of individuals like Alex, a graphic designer, the creative peaks associated with manic episodes also bring heightened impulsivity, testing personal and professional bonds. Through the lens of Alex's experiences, we see the critical role of therapy and open communication in navigating these complexities, enabling him to maintain meaningful relationships and pursue his career ambitions. His story is one of learning and adaptation, reflecting the broader theme of balancing life's demands with the management of bipolar disorder.

Conversely, Jamie's narrative sheds light on the societal stigma that often shadows bipolar disorder. As a university lecturer, Jamie encountered misunderstanding and isolation due to misconceptions about her condition. Yet, by channeling her experiences into advocacy and education, she not only confronts this stigma but also carves out a space for empowerment and community building, highlighting the transformative power of sharing one's journey.

These narratives, among countless others, reflect the multifaceted reality of living with bipolar disorder. They underscore the message that, despite its challenges, bipolar disorder also presents opportunities for personal growth, resilience, and achievement. With the right combination of support, management strategies, and self-awareness, individuals with bipolar disorder can navigate their condition successfully, leading rich and rewarding lives.

CHAPTER 2

Treatment and Management Strategies

The journey towards managing bipolar disorder encompasses a spectrum of effective strategies. This chapter explores essential components ranging from medication choices and their impacts to psychotherapeutic methods tailored for this condition. The aim is to provide a thorough overview of available treatments, highlighting how they can be personalized to meet the individual needs of those living with bipolar disorder.

Additionally, this chapter underscores the significance of lifestyle adjustments and proactive crisis management in maintaining equilibrium. The supportive role of networks—comprising family, friends, and professionals—is also examined, showcasing their critical contribution to the success of treatment plans and overall well-being.

Medications

The treatment of bipolar disorder involves a sophisticated pharmacological strategy aimed at stabilizing mood swings and preventing relapse. Central to this approach are mood stabilizers, atypical antipsychotics, and, in some cases, antidepressants. Each category of medication serves a unique function in correcting the neurochemical disparities linked to bipolar disorder, providing a stable base for ongoing mental wellness.

Mood Stabilizers

Mood stabilizers constitute the cornerstone of medication options for managing bipolar disorder, aimed primarily at preventing the extreme highs of mania and the debilitating lows of depression that characterize the condition. Among these, lithium stands out for its long-standing use and effectiveness in both controlling acute manic episodes and serving as a preventive measure against future episodes. Its exact mechanism of action remains not fully elucidated, but it's believed to stabilize mood by influencing multiple neurotransmitter systems and modulating the second messenger systems within neurons.

Another widely used mood stabilizer is valproate, which is often preferred for rapid-cycling bipolar disorder and mixed states, offering significant mood stabilization by enhancing GABA (gamma-aminobutyric acid) levels in the brain and modulating glutamate neurotransmission. Lamotrigine, notable for its efficacy in the management of bipolar depression, works differently, inhibiting voltage-sensitive sodium channels and thereby stabilizing neuronal membranes.

The prescription of mood stabilizers requires a nuanced understanding of their potential side effects and the need for regular monitoring to ensure both efficacy and safety. Lithium, for instance, necessitates close monitoring of blood levels to avoid toxicity, with potential side effects including kidney function impairment, thyroid abnormalities, and tremors. Valproate's side effects may include weight gain, hair loss, and possible liver damage, underscoring the importance of liver function tests during treatment.

Lamotrigine, while generally well-tolerated, carries a risk for skin rash, which can be serious in rare cases. The management of side effects, coupled with the careful titration of doses to the individual's response, underscores the dynamic process of finding the optimal therapeutic regimen for each person with bipolar disorder.

Atypical Antipsychotics

Atypical antipsychotics have become a pivotal component in the pharmacological arsenal against bipolar disorder, particularly valuable for their efficacy in treating manic episodes and, for some, depressive episodes or as maintenance therapy to prevent recurrence. These medications, including olanzapine, quetiapine, risperidone, and aripiprazole, distinguish themselves from their first-generation counterparts by offering a broader spectrum of neurotransmitter target engagement, including dopamine and serotonin receptors, which contributes to their mood-stabilizing effects.

Their action mechanism involves the modulation of these neurotransmitter systems to reduce the severity of manic symptoms and help stabilize mood fluctuations inherent in bipolar disorder. For instance, quetiapine is often utilized for its effectiveness in treating both manic and depressive episodes, making it a versatile option for those with bipolar disorder, while aripiprazole is noted for its preventive capabilities against manic episodes when used as part of maintenance therapy.

While atypical antipsychotics represent a significant advancement in treating bipolar disorder, their use must be carefully managed due to potential side effects. Common concerns with these medications include weight gain, the development of metabolic syndrome, and extrapyramidal symptoms, though the risk and severity of these side effects vary widely among the different atypical antipsychotics. For example, olanzapine is particularly associated with weight gain and changes in metabolism, necessitating regular monitoring of blood glucose and lipid levels for patients on this medication.

Conversely, aripiprazole tends to have a more favorable side effect profile, with lower risks of weight gain and metabolic complications, making it a preferred choice for long-term maintenance in some patients. The management of side effects is a critical aspect of treatment with atypical antipsychotics, requiring ongoing assessment and adjustments by healthcare providers to ensure that the benefits of treatment outweigh the risks. This balance is crucial for optimizing the quality of life and treatment adherence among individuals with bipolar disorder, underscoring the need for a personalized approach to medication management.

Antidepressants

Antidepressants, while used with caution, play a nuanced role in the treatment arsenal for bipolar disorder, primarily targeting the depressive phases that can be profoundly debilitating for individuals with the condition. Their application in bipolar disorder treatment is delicate due to the risk of precipitating manic or hypomanic episodes, a phenomenon known as "mood switching." Therefore, antidepressants are typically prescribed in conjunction with a mood stabilizer or atypical antipsychotic to mitigate this risk.

Among the classes of antidepressants, Selective Serotonin Reuptake Inhibitors (SSRIs) and Serotonin-Norepinephrine Reuptake Inhibitors (SNRIs) are commonly utilized for their efficacy and relatively favorable side effect profile. SSRIs, such as fluoxetine and sertraline, increase serotonin levels in the brain, potentially improving mood and alleviating depressive symptoms. SNRIs, including venlafaxine and duloxetine, target both serotonin and norepinephrine, offering another therapeutic avenue for depression in bipolar disorder, with attention to balancing mood stabilization.

The use of antidepressants in bipolar disorder necessitates a strategic and informed approach, underscored by the importance of close monitoring for any signs of mood destabilization. The decision to incorporate an antidepressant into a treatment plan is grounded in a comprehensive assessment of the individual's history with depressive episodes, previous treatment responses, and current symptomatology.

Bupropion is another antidepressant option considered for its dopaminergic and noradrenergic mechanisms, which may be less likely to trigger manic episodes compared to other antidepressants, though clinical vigilance remains paramount. Managing the potential side effects of antidepressants, which can range from gastrointestinal disturbances to increased anxiety and sleep issues, is critical for maintaining overall treatment adherence and patient well-being.

Combination Therapy and Medication Management

Combination therapy and medication management form the bedrock of effective bipolar disorder treatment, recognizing that a multifaceted approach is often necessary to address the complexity of the condition. Combination therapy involves the concurrent use of multiple medications, such as mood stabilizers, atypical antipsychotics, and sometimes antidepressants, to target the diverse symptoms of bipolar disorder. This method is predicated on the understanding that bipolar disorder's manic and depressive episodes might not be fully managed by a single medication.

For instance, a mood stabilizer may be prescribed to control manic episodes, while an atypical antipsychotic could be added to enhance mood stabilization and address psychotic symptoms, if present. Additionally, an antidepressant might be introduced for significant depressive episodes, always with caution to avoid triggering mania. The synergy between different medications aims to provide a more comprehensive coverage of symptoms, enhancing overall mood stability and improving the quality of life for individuals with bipolar disorder.

Effective medication management within combination therapy is crucial, involving meticulous titration of dosages, monitoring for side effects, and adjusting the regimen as needed based on the individual's response to treatment. The process begins with careful selection and dosing of medications, followed by close observation for therapeutic effectiveness and adverse effects.

This dynamic process requires regular follow-ups with healthcare providers to assess the treatment's impact and make necessary adjustments. For example, the dosage of a mood stabilizer may be gradually increased to find the optimal therapeutic dose, while minimizing side effects. Similarly, if a patient experiences significant side effects from an atypical antipsychotic, a switch to another medication within the same class with a more tolerable side effect profile may be considered.

Understanding and Managing Side Effects

Understanding and managing side effects is a critical aspect of medication treatment for bipolar disorder, as it directly impacts patient adherence, overall well-being, and the effectiveness of the treatment plan. Medications used in treating bipolar disorder, including mood stabilizers, atypical antipsychotics, and antidepressants, come with a range of potential side effects. These can vary from relatively mild, such as minor gastrointestinal discomfort or temporary sedation, to more serious concerns like weight gain, metabolic syndrome, extrapyramidal symptoms, or long-term organ function impacts.

For example, lithium, a cornerstone mood stabilizer for bipolar disorder, may cause thyroid and kidney function alterations over time, necessitating regular monitoring. Atypical antipsychotics, while effective for manic and depressive episodes, can lead to significant weight gain and changes in glucose and lipid metabolism, increasing the risk of diabetes and cardiovascular disease. Antidepressants used cautiously, can sometimes induce mania or accelerate cycling patterns. Understanding these side effects allows patients and healthcare providers to navigate the treatment process more effectively, ensuring that the benefits of any medication outweigh its risks.

Managing these side effects involves a proactive and collaborative approach between the patient and their healthcare team, emphasizing open communication, regular monitoring, and lifestyle adjustments. Regular blood tests, weight monitoring, and discussions about how the medication feels are integral parts of this process. When side effects are identified, adjustments to the treatment regimen may be necessary, which can include dose modifications, switching to a medication with a more favorable side effect profile, or introducing additional treatments to counteract specific side effects.

For instance, adding a medication to manage metabolic side effects of atypical antipsychotics, or utilizing beta-blockers to counteract tremors associated with lithium. Additionally, incorporating lifestyle interventions such as dietary counseling, exercise programs, and sleep hygiene practices can mitigate some medication side effects, enhancing overall physical health and treatment tolerance. Ultimately, the goal is to achieve a balance where the medication provides maximum therapeutic benefit with minimal side effects, fostering sustained adherence to treatment and improving the quality of life for individuals with bipolar disorder.

Advocating for Your Health

Advocating for your health in the context of bipolar disorder medication treatment is a crucial aspect of navigating the path to wellness. It involves becoming an informed participant in your care, actively engaging in discussions with healthcare providers about treatment options, and voicing concerns and preferences regarding medication. This empowerment is essential because medication strategies for bipolar disorder are highly personalized, varying significantly from one individual to another based on their symptom profile, side effects tolerance, and lifestyle.

Patients who educate themselves about the different medications, how they work, possible side effects, and the significance of following their treatment plan closely are more prepared to work together with their healthcare professionals to make choices that support their treatment objectives. Advocacy also means communicating effectively about how the medication impacts daily living, including any side effects experienced, to ensure the treatment plan remains responsive to the patient's evolving needs.

Furthermore, advocating for one's health extends beyond the clinical setting into daily life, where individuals must navigate the complexities of medication adherence, lifestyle adjustments, and self-monitoring for symptom changes or side effects. It involves developing a support network that includes family, friends, and possibly peer support groups, all of which can provide encouragement and understanding throughout the treatment journey.

Learning to advocate for oneself also means recognizing when to seek additional help or a second opinion, particularly if treatment outcomes are not as expected or if side effects become challenging to manage. By taking an active role in their treatment, individuals with bipolar disorder can foster a sense of agency and control over their condition, leading to more positive health outcomes and an enhanced feeling of contentment with their care.

Understanding the pharmacological landscape for treating bipolar disorder is vital for anyone navigating this condition. With a comprehensive knowledge of medication options, their effects, and how to manage them, individuals with bipolar disorder can advocate for their health and work collaboratively with their care providers to achieve optimal treatment outcomes. The goal is to empower patients to manage their condition with confidence, ensuring a partnership in care that respects their experiences and prioritizes their mental and physical health.

Psychotherapy Techniques for Bipolar Disorder

Psychotherapy plays a pivotal role in the comprehensive management of bipolar disorder, offering individuals tools and strategies to cope with the disorder beyond pharmacological treatments. Various psychotherapeutic interventions have been tailored to meet the unique needs of those living with bipolar disorder, each with specific goals and mechanisms of action. Understanding these can empower individuals to navigate their condition more effectively and can complement their overall treatment plan for a holistic approach to managing bipolar disorder.

Cognitive-Behavioral Therapy (CBT)

Cognitive-Behavioral Therapy (CBT) stands as a highly effective psychotherapy technique for managing bipolar disorder, primarily focusing on identifying and modifying dysfunctional thought patterns and behaviors that contribute to the cyclical nature of the condition. Central to CBT is the premise that negative thought patterns and maladaptive behaviors can significantly influence mood states, potentially triggering manic or depressive episodes.

Through CBT, individuals with bipolar disorder are taught to recognize these harmful thoughts and behaviors and are equipped with strategies to challenge and change them. For instance, a patient might learn to identify automatic negative thoughts that emerge during a depressive phase, such as feelings of worthlessness or hopelessness, and use cognitive restructuring techniques to replace these thoughts with more balanced, realistic perspectives. This process not only aids in alleviating depressive symptoms but also fosters a more resilient mindset against future episodes.

Moreover, CBT for bipolar disorder includes behavioral activation techniques aimed at encouraging patients to engage in activities that can enhance their mood and overall well-being. This aspect of CBT is particularly crucial during depressive episodes when motivation and energy levels are low. Patients are guided to set achievable goals, gradually increasing their engagement in positive activities, thereby disrupting the cycle of depression and inactivity.

Additionally, CBT therapists work with individuals to develop effective coping strategies for dealing with stress and managing triggers that could lead to mood episodes. Skills such as problem-solving, stress management, and mindfulness are integrated into the therapy, providing a comprehensive toolkit that supports the long-term management of the disorder. Through regular sessions, homework assignments, and continuous collaboration between the patient and therapist, CBT empowers individuals with bipolar disorder to take an active role in their treatment, leading to improved mood stability and a reduced risk of relapse.

Dialectical Behavior Therapy (DBT)

Dialectical Behavior Therapy (DBT) has been increasingly recognized as a valuable psychotherapy technique for individuals with bipolar disorder, particularly for those who experience intense emotional turmoil and impulsivity. Originally developed to treat borderline personality disorder, DBT's principles and techniques have been effectively adapted to address the emotional dysregulation and distress tolerance challenges commonly faced by those with bipolar disorder. Fundamentally, DBT is centered around the concept of balancing the acceptance of one's emotions and experiences with the effort to change.

The therapy highlights four main skills: mindfulness, the ability to tolerate distress, regulating emotions, and enhancing interpersonal effectiveness. Mindfulness practices within DBT teach individuals to remain present and fully aware of the moment, helping to reduce the overwhelming emotions that can lead to mood swings. Distress tolerance skills are aimed at enhancing the ability to tolerate and survive crises without resorting to self-destructive behaviors that can exacerbate the condition.

Emotion regulation is another critical component of DBT, offering strategies to identify and manage intense emotions without being overwhelmed by them, thereby reducing the frequency and severity of mood episodes. This includes understanding the triggers of emotional responses and learning to apply techniques to prevent or reduce emotional intensity. Interpersonal effectiveness skills in DBT focus on improving relationships and communication, which can often be strained by the symptoms of bipolar disorder. Patients learn to assert their needs and manage conflicts in a healthy, constructive manner, fostering better personal and professional relationships.

Through a combination of individual therapy, group skills training sessions, and as-needed coaching, DBT provides a structured environment in which individuals with bipolar disorder can develop the skills necessary to manage their condition more effectively. This comprehensive approach not only addresses the symptoms of bipolar disorder but also builds a foundation for lasting emotional resilience and stability, empowering patients to lead more fulfilling lives.

Psychoeducation

Psychoeducation as a psychotherapeutic technique for bipolar disorder serves an essential function by empowering patients and their families with knowledge about the condition, its treatment options, and effective management strategies. This educational approach demystifies the disorder, providing a solid foundation of understanding that can significantly impact treatment adherence, reduce relapse rates, and improve overall outcomes.

By informing patients about the nature of bipolar disorder, including its symptoms, causes, and course, psychoeducation helps individuals recognize the importance of maintaining their treatment regimen, identifying early warning signs of mood episodes, and understanding the impact of lifestyle factors on their condition. Additionally, psychoeducation sessions often cover effective coping mechanisms and stress management techniques, equipping patients with practical tools to manage their condition proactively.

This knowledge fosters a sense of agency and control over their disorder, encouraging active participation in their care. Beyond the individual, psychoeducation extends to family members and close friends, involving them in the therapeutic process. This inclusion is crucial, as it builds a supportive network around the patient, enhancing the understanding and empathy of those closest to them. For families, psychoeducation offers insights into how best to support their loved one, including how to communicate effectively, how to respond to mood episodes constructively, and how to maintain a stable and supportive home environment.

The technique can be delivered through various formats, including group sessions, workshops, and digital platforms, making it accessible and engaging. By fostering a collaborative and informed approach to managing bipolar disorder, psychoeducation bridges the gap between clinical treatment and daily living, ensuring that patients and their support networks are well-equipped to face the challenges of the disorder together.

Family Therapy

Family therapy emerges as a critical psychotherapy technique in managing bipolar disorder, recognizing the profound impact the condition has not only on the individuals diagnosed but also on their families. This therapeutic approach centers on enhancing communication, understanding, and support within the family unit, providing members with the tools to navigate the complexities of bipolar disorder together. Through family therapy, all members learn about the nature of bipolar disorder, its effects on mood and behavior, and the importance of a supportive environment for managing the condition.

Sessions are designed to foster open dialogue, enabling family members to express their concerns, experiences, and feelings in a safe and structured setting. This process helps to alleviate misunderstandings and resolve conflicts that may arise from the challenges of living with bipolar disorder. Additionally, family therapy aims to strengthen the family's problem-solving abilities, teaching strategies for dealing with stressors and changes in the affected member's mood.

Beyond improving communication and conflict resolution, family therapy plays a vital role in building a cohesive support network that can significantly reduce relapse rates and promote sustained recovery. Therapists guide families in identifying and implementing effective support strategies, such as establishing routines that encourage stability, setting realistic expectations, and recognizing the early signs of mood episodes.

Moreover, family members learn how to maintain their well-being, ensuring that the care they provide is sustainable and does not lead to caregiver burnout. By equipping families with a deeper understanding of bipolar disorder and practical skills for day-to-day management, family therapy enhances the resilience of both the individual with the disorder and their family. This collaborative approach not only supports the treatment goals of the individual with bipolar disorder but also fosters a nurturing home environment conducive to long-term wellness and mutual growth.

Interpersonal and Social Rhythm Therapy (IPSRT)

Interpersonal and Social Rhythm Therapy (IPSRT) is a distinctive psychotherapy technique designed specifically for the treatment of bipolar disorder, with a dual focus on stabilizing daily routines and improving interpersonal relationships. The core premise of IPSRT is that disruptions in daily rhythms, including sleep, eating patterns, and physical activity, can precipitate or exacerbate mood episodes in individuals with bipolar disorder.

By helping patients establish and maintain regular daily routines, IPSRT aims to reduce the frequency and severity of these episodes. This therapy integrates principles from interpersonal psychotherapy, addressing issues such as role transitions, grief, interpersonal disputes, and social isolation, which are known to impact mood stability. Through IPSRT, patients learn to recognize the interplay between their social environment and mood regulation, developing strategies to minimize stressors and enhance their ability to maintain consistent social rhythms.

Furthermore, IPSRT places significant emphasis on the identification and management of personal triggers that disrupt social rhythms, such as travel across time zones, irregular work schedules, or interpersonal conflicts. Patients work closely with therapists to develop personalized strategies for anticipating and managing these disruptions, incorporating techniques to improve sleep hygiene, establish regular meal times, and engage in consistent physical activity.

The therapeutic process also involves building skills to enhance communication and assertiveness in relationships, empowering patients to navigate social interactions more effectively and advocate for their needs. By fostering a stable daily routine and enhancing interpersonal skills, IPSRT contributes to improved mood regulation and overall well-being for individuals with bipolar disorder. This approach not only addresses the immediate symptoms of the disorder but also builds a foundation for long-term management, emphasizing the critical role of structure and support in achieving and maintaining mood stability.

Each of these psychotherapeutic approaches offers valuable tools and insights for individuals with bipolar disorder, contributing to a comprehensive treatment plan that addresses the condition's complexity. By incorporating psychotherapy into their care, individuals with bipolar disorder can gain a deeper understanding of their condition, develop effective coping strategies, and build networks of support that improve their life quality and capacity to handle the disorder. Through a combination of pharmacological treatment and psychotherapy, individuals with bipolar disorder can work towards achieving stability, improving their relationships, and leading fulfilling lives.

Lifestyle Modifications

Integrating healthy lifestyle choices constitutes a foundational element in managing bipolar disorder comprehensively. This multi-faceted approach, grounded in the synergy between nutritional psychiatry, regular physical activity, and stringent sleep hygiene practices, not only augments traditional medication and psychotherapy but also empowers individuals with actionable strategies for enhancing mental health.

Nutritional Psychiatry and Diet

Nutritional psychiatry underscores the significant relationship between diet and mental health, particularly in the context of managing bipolar disorder. This emerging field suggests that what we consume can profoundly impact our brain chemistry, mood stability, and overall well-being. For individuals with bipolar disorder, adopting a diet rich in specific nutrients can play a pivotal role in mitigating mood swings and enhancing treatment outcomes. Foods high in omega-3 fatty acids, such as fatty fish, flaxseeds, and walnuts, are of particular interest due to their potential to stabilize mood.

These essential fats contribute to the maintenance of cell membrane integrity in brain cells, facilitating smoother neurotransmission, which is crucial for mood regulation. Additionally, diets that emphasize whole grains, lean proteins, and a variety of fruits and vegetables can ensure a steady supply of antioxidants, vitamins, and minerals that support brain health. These nutritional choices help combat oxidative stress—a condition linked to mood disorders—and promote overall neurological well-being.

Beyond the basics of a balanced diet, individuals with bipolar disorder might also benefit from paying attention to dietary patterns that influence the gut-brain axis. Emerging research highlights the role of gut health in mood regulation, pointing to the benefits of incorporating probiotic and prebiotic foods, such as yogurt, kefir, and high-fiber foods, to support a healthy gut microbiome. Attention to the timing of meals and the composition of macronutrients can also affect mood stability; for example, regular, balanced meals can prevent blood sugar spikes and dips that may trigger mood changes.

However, it's essential to approach dietary changes with mindfulness and ideally under the guidance of healthcare professionals, such as dietitians specializing in psychiatric conditions, to tailor dietary interventions to individual health needs and preferences. Through a comprehensive approach to nutrition, individuals living with bipolar disorder can harness the power of their diet to support their mental health, contributing to a holistic strategy for managing the condition alongside medication and psychotherapy.

Physical Activity

Physical activity is increasingly recognized as a critical component of a comprehensive treatment plan for bipolar disorder, offering a natural and accessible means to enhance mental health alongside traditional medication and psychotherapy approaches. Engaging in regular exercise has been shown to have a profound impact on brain chemistry, particularly in its ability to increase the production of endorphins, sometimes referred to as the body's natural mood lifters. These biochemical changes can help alleviate symptoms of depression and, to some extent, contribute to the stabilization of manic episodes.

Furthermore, exercise promotes the release of neurotrophic factors, such as Brain-Derived Neurotrophic Factor (BDNF), which supports brain health, neural plasticity, and overall cognitive function. Regular physical activity also helps regulate sleep patterns and circadian rhythms, both of which are often disrupted in individuals with bipolar disorder, leading to mood instability. The benefits extend to improving energy levels, increasing self-esteem, and reducing anxiety, all contributing to a higher quality of life.

Tailoring an exercise regimen to fit the individual's current physical condition, interests, and mood state is crucial to ensuring sustained engagement and maximizing the therapeutic benefits. For those with bipolar disorder, this might mean choosing low-impact, rhythmic activities such as walking, cycling, or swimming during depressive phases to boost energy and mood gradually. During more stable periods, incorporating a mix of cardiovascular exercise, strength training, and flexibility exercises can enhance physical health and resilience against mood swings.

Individuals need to monitor their response to exercise closely, as too much physical activity during manic phases could potentially exacerbate symptoms. Working with healthcare professionals, including psychiatrists and physical therapists, can help individuals with bipolar disorder develop a balanced and safe exercise plan. Encouraging gradual increases in activity levels, setting realistic goals, and identifying enjoyable forms of exercise can foster a positive and lasting relationship with physical activity as a vital tool in managing bipolar disorder.

Sleep Hygiene

Sleep hygiene plays a crucial role in the management of bipolar disorder, given the intricate link between sleep patterns and mood regulation. Disruptions in sleep, such as insomnia during manic episodes or hypersomnia during depressive phases, can significantly impact the course of the disorder, often precipitating mood episodes or exacerbating existing symptoms. Implementing good sleep hygiene practices involves creating a conducive sleep environment and establishing routines that promote consistent, restorative sleep.

Key strategies include adhering to a regular sleep schedule, even on weekends, to regulate the body's internal clock; creating a bedtime ritual that signals the brain it's time to wind down, such as reading or a warm bath; and ensuring the sleep environment is cool, quiet, and comfortable. Minimizing exposure to screens and blue light from electronics before bedtime is also essential, as they can interfere with the production of melatonin, the hormone responsible for sleep regulation.

Beyond physical preparations, cognitive-behavioral techniques for insomnia (CBT-I) can be particularly beneficial for individuals with bipolar disorder, offering strategies to combat the negative thought patterns that often accompany attempts to fall asleep. For example, CBT-I techniques might involve learning to associate the bed with sleep only (not work or entertainment), thereby strengthening the mental association between bed and sleep. Managing caffeine intake and avoiding heavy meals or vigorous exercise close to bedtime are additional practical steps that can improve sleep quality.

Given the potential for certain bipolar disorder medications to affect sleep, open communication with healthcare providers about the impact of medication on sleep patterns is vital. Adjustments to medication timing or the introduction of sleep-promoting medications may sometimes be necessary, always under the guidance of a healthcare professional. Emphasizing sleep hygiene within the broader context of bipolar disorder management underscores the importance of sleep in maintaining mental health stability and overall well-being.

Implementing Sustainable Lifestyle Changes

Adapting to sustainable lifestyle changes significantly bolsters the management of bipolar disorder, emphasizing the necessity for a holistic and personalized approach to health. The journey towards these changes begins with recognizing the profound impact that habits related to diet, exercise, and sleep have on mood stability and overall well-being. Sustainable implementation means adopting modifications that are not only beneficial in the short term but are also viable and enjoyable long-term practices.

This often involves setting realistic, achievable goals that motivate continued effort without causing undue stress or feelings of failure. For instance, gradually incorporating more nutrient-dense foods into the diet, finding physical activities that bring joy and can be consistently engaged in, and establishing a bedtime routine that promotes restful sleep are steps that contribute to a holistic strategy for managing bipolar disorder. The essence of sustainability lies in the balance—making changes that are significant enough to have a positive impact, yet flexible enough to be maintained over time and adapted as circumstances change.

Beyond the initial steps of making lifestyle changes, ongoing support and education play vital roles in maintaining these habits. Regular check-ins with healthcare providers, including psychiatrists, dietitians, and physical therapists, can provide guidance, monitor progress, and adjust plans as needed. Support groups, whether in-person or online, offer a community of individuals facing similar challenges, providing encouragement and sharing strategies that have been effective in their own lives. Educating oneself about bipolar disorder and understanding how various lifestyle factors influence the condition empowers individuals to make informed decisions about their care.

Encouragement to persist with these changes, even in the face of setbacks, is crucial, as is celebrating successes, no matter how small they may seem. Ultimately, implementing sustainable lifestyle changes in the management of bipolar disorder is an evolving process that requires patience, support, and a commitment to self-care, laying the foundation for improved health and stability.

By embracing these lifestyle modifications, individuals with bipolar disorder are equipped with a comprehensive toolkit for navigating the condition, enhancing traditional treatment modalities, and promoting a robust mental health framework.

Crisis Management: Developing a Plan for Acute Episodes

Creating a comprehensive crisis management plan is an essential component of living with bipolar disorder, ensuring that individuals and their support networks are prepared for acute episodes with a structured response strategy. This plan encompasses recognizing early warning signs, implementing immediate coping mechanisms, and effectively engaging healthcare professionals and caregivers to mitigate the impact of the episode.

Identifying Early Warning Signs

Identifying early warning signs is a critical first step in the effective crisis management of bipolar disorder, serving as the foundation for preemptive action and intervention before an acute episode fully manifests. These warning signs can be subtle or pronounced changes in an individual's thoughts, feelings, behaviors, or physical state, signaling an impending shift towards either a manic or depressive episode. For many, these signs might include alterations in sleep patterns, such as difficulty falling asleep or sleeping too much, changes in appetite or energy levels, increased irritability, or a noticeable decline in interest in daily activities.

Others might experience heightened anxiety, rapid speech, restlessness, or a surge in ambitious projects or ideas as precursors to a manic episode. Conversely, warning signs for a depressive episode might encompass persistent sadness, withdrawal from social interactions, a marked decrease in productivity, or pervasive feelings of hopelessness. Recognizing these signs requires individuals to maintain a high degree of self-awareness and, often, to keep a detailed journal or mood chart to track fluctuations in mood, thoughts, and behaviors over time.

Equally important in identifying early warning signs is the role of the support network, including family members, friends, and healthcare providers, who can often observe shifts in behavior or mood that the individual might not recognize. Training this support network to identify and respond appropriately to these warning signs is a crucial component of a comprehensive crisis management plan. It involves open and ongoing communication about the nature of these signs and how they manifest for the individual, fostering a shared understanding and readiness to act.

This collaborative approach ensures that, at the first indication of an impending episode, a support system is in place to offer immediate assistance, whether that means providing emotional support, helping to adjust the environment to reduce stressors, or facilitating contact with healthcare providers to reassess and adjust treatment plans as necessary. Through the early identification of warning signs and a coordinated response strategy, individuals with bipolar disorder and their support networks can significantly mitigate the severity of acute episodes, paving the way for a more stable and manageable course of the condition.

Practical Steps for Escalating Symptoms

When symptoms of bipolar disorder begin to escalate, having a concrete, actionable plan in place is crucial to prevent the progression into a full-blown manic or depressive episode. Practical steps for dealing with escalating symptoms are centered around immediate interventions that can be initiated by the individual or their support network.

One of the first steps is to utilize established coping strategies that have been effective in the past, such as engaging in mindfulness or relaxation techniques, initiating light physical activity, or employing distraction methods like reading or listening to calming music. These activities can serve as immediate buffers to rising stress levels and symptomatic escalation. Simultaneously, it's vital to assess the environment and remove or mitigate any potential stressors that could exacerbate the situation, such as postponing stressful tasks or avoiding conflict situations.

In tandem with these initial interventions, communication with healthcare providers should be prioritized. This might involve reaching out to a psychiatrist or therapist to discuss the escalating symptoms and consider adjustments to the treatment plan, such as medication changes or additional therapy sessions. If symptoms continue to intensify despite these measures, it may be necessary to seek emergency medical help or hospitalization as a precautionary step to ensure safety and stabilize the condition.

In such situations, having a pre-prepared emergency contact list and a medical information packet can streamline the process and ensure that the individual receives the appropriate care promptly. These practical steps form the core of a responsive strategy to manage escalating symptoms in bipolar disorder, emphasizing the importance of early intervention, support, and professional guidance to navigate through crisis situations effectively.

Involving Healthcare Team and Support Network

Involving the healthcare team and support network is a fundamental aspect of managing a crisis plan for acute episodes of bipolar disorder. This collaborative approach ensures that individuals have a comprehensive safety net that integrates professional medical advice with emotional and practical support from loved ones. Effective communication with healthcare professionals, such as psychiatrists, psychologists, and therapists, allows for the rapid adjustment of treatment plans in response to escalating symptoms.

This might include changes in medication, emergency therapy sessions, or hospitalization if deemed necessary. By keeping the healthcare team informed about any changes in mood or behavior, individuals can receive timely interventions that may prevent a full crisis. Additionally, healthcare providers can offer guidance to the support network on how to best assist during these times, ensuring actions taken are conducive to the individual's recovery.

The support network, consisting of family, friends, and possibly peers from support groups, plays a crucial role in providing a comforting presence and practical assistance during challenging periods. Educating this network about bipolar disorder, including warning signs of escalating symptoms and how to respond effectively, empowers them to act swiftly and appropriately. Whether it's providing transportation to medical appointments, ensuring the individual is not alone during vulnerable times, or simply offering a listening ear, the support network's involvement is invaluable.

Establishing clear communication channels and roles can help distribute responsibilities, preventing caregiver burnout and ensuring the individual receives holistic support. This concerted effort between the healthcare team and the support network forms the backbone of a robust crisis management plan, highlighting the importance of a united front in navigating the turbulent waters of bipolar disorder with resilience and hope.

Legal Considerations and Advance Directives

Legal considerations and advance directives play a crucial role in the comprehensive management of bipolar disorder, especially when developing a plan for managing acute episodes. These legal tools ensure that an individual's treatment preferences are respected and followed, even during periods when they might not be able to communicate their wishes directly due to the severity of their symptoms. Advance directives for health care, often part of a broader psychiatric advance directive (PAD), allow individuals with bipolar disorder to document their treatment preferences, including medications, hospitalization options, and even preferences for doctors and healthcare facilities, for times when they are in crisis.

This preemptive legal preparation empowers patients, giving them a voice in their treatment process and offering peace of mind that their care aligns with their values and wishes. Additionally, designating a durable power of attorney for healthcare decisions is a critical step, enabling a trusted family member, friend, or advocate to make healthcare decisions on the individual's behalf if they become incapacitated. This designated agent is typically someone who understands the individual's treatment preferences well and is committed to ensuring that those preferences are honored.

The creation and implementation of advance directives require thoughtful consideration and often the assistance of a legal professional knowledgeable in mental health law. It's essential for individuals with bipolar disorder to discuss their wishes and instructions with their healthcare team and designated healthcare proxy to ensure clarity and understanding. Regular reviews and updates of these documents are advisable, as treatment preferences and personal circumstances may evolve.

Furthermore, making these documents readily accessible to the designated healthcare proxy and relevant medical professionals is paramount to ensure that the directives are followed during a crisis. By integrating legal considerations and advance directives into the crisis management plan, individuals with bipolar disorder can exert greater control over their treatment journey, ensuring that decisions made during acute episodes are in line with their long-term health goals and personal values.

Utilization of Templates, Checklists, and Personal Narratives

In the context of crisis management for bipolar disorder, the utilization of templates, checklists, and personal narratives plays a vital role in streamlining the response process during acute episodes. Templates and checklists serve as ready references that outline specific steps to be taken when warning signs of a potential crisis appear. These tools can include detailed action plans for escalating symptoms, emergency contact information, medication lists with dosages, and individualized coping strategies.

The advantage of having such resources at hand is the reduction of decision-making stress during high-anxiety periods, ensuring that both the individual with bipolar disorder and their support network can act quickly and effectively. Moreover, checklists can facilitate communication with healthcare providers by providing clear and concise information about the individual's current condition, treatment history, and any recent changes in medication or symptoms.

Personal narratives, on the other hand, offer powerful insights and relatable experiences that can guide individuals through their crisis management efforts. Take, for example, the practical application of these tools in Sarah's life, a scenario that many might find relatable. Sarah, who navigates the challenges of bipolar disorder, has meticulously developed a crisis management plan, central to which is a checklist that outlines steps from recognizing early symptoms to engaging her support network and healthcare team.

Her checklist begins with recognizing early warning signs, such as a decreased need for sleep or an unusual increase in energy levels, prompting her to engage in predefined calming activities like meditation or journaling. When these signs intensify, Sarah knows it's time to reach out to her support system, a step clearly outlined in her plan. This action was crucial one evening when Sarah felt her thoughts racing faster than usual, and her energy levels were inexplicably high, signaling the onset of a manic episode. She immediately turned to her checklist, contacting her brother, who was informed and ready to help because Sarah had shared her crisis management plan with him beforehand. Together, they contacted her healthcare provider, who had been part of creating the plan, to adjust her treatment temporarily.

Sarah's story is a testament to the effectiveness of integrating structured tools like checklists and templates with the personal touch of narratives in managing bipolar disorder. Her experience illustrates not just the steps taken during a crisis but the emotional journey, challenges, and the sense of empowerment that comes from having a plan. This holistic approach, blending practical strategies with personal experiences, underscores the value of comprehensive planning in fostering resilience and stability for individuals with bipolar disorder.

In crafting a detailed crisis management plan, individuals with bipolar disorder empower themselves and their support systems to handle acute episodes with informed confidence. This comprehensive approach not only safeguards against the escalation of symptoms but also underscores the importance of preparedness, support, and proactive management in the journey toward long-term stability and well-being.

The Role of Support Networks in Treatment Success

In the nuanced journey of managing bipolar disorder, the significance of a robust support network—encompassing family, friends, and peer groups—becomes a cornerstone of effective treatment and overall wellness. This intricate web of support plays a multifaceted role, offering emotional solace, practical aid, and a shared understanding that can significantly lighten the burden of the disorder. Creating an environment replete with support and understanding requires concerted efforts, emphasizing the cultivation of open communication, the establishment of healthy boundaries, and an unwavering commitment to mutual respect and care.

Families and friends are often at the frontline, navigating the complexities of bipolar disorder alongside their loved ones. Their involvement extends from providing a listening ear to actively participating in treatment plans, advocating for their loved ones, and sometimes, intervening during crises. This level of engagement necessitates a deep understanding of bipolar disorder, which is fostered through education and dialogue.

Learning about the disorder's manifestations, treatment options, and coping mechanisms equips supporters with the knowledge to offer meaningful assistance. Furthermore, engaging in open communication channels allows for the expression of needs, concerns, and feelings, facilitating a collaborative approach to management. Within this dynamic, setting healthy boundaries is crucial. These boundaries ensure that the support provided is respectful of the individual's autonomy and promotes independence rather than dependency.

Support groups, both virtual and physical, extend the reach of this support network, offering a platform for exchanging experiences, strategies, and encouragement. These groups serve as a testament to the power of community, offering perspectives that may broaden an individual's understanding of their condition and introducing coping strategies that others have found effective. The benefits of such communal support are reciprocal; individuals gain insights and reassurance, while also providing the same to others, fostering a nurturing circle of support.

Moreover, the importance of self-care for caregivers is highlighted within these networks. The emotional toll of caring for someone with bipolar disorder can be significant, making self-care an essential practice for maintaining one's health and well-being. Professional support for families, through avenues like family therapy, further underscores the value of a comprehensive support system. These services can help resolve conflicts, improve communication, and strengthen the family unit, creating a more supportive environment for managing bipolar disorder.

Narratives of individuals and their journeys with bipolar disorder, supported by their networks, illustrate the transformative impact of such support. Consider the story of Carl, whose early signs of a depressive episode were swiftly recognized by his sister, thanks to their open communication and her understanding of his condition.

Her timely intervention and coordination with his healthcare provider averted a deeper crisis. Or the story of Lena, who found solace and strength in her online support group, a community that offered her practical advice and emotional support during her most challenging times. These stories embody the essence of collaborative care in bipolar disorder management, showcasing how empowered, informed support networks can significantly influence treatment outcomes and quality of life.

These narratives, alongside expert advice and practical strategies, underscore the significance of building and nurturing support networks. Such communities are not just beneficial but essential in the holistic management of bipolar disorder. They embody the collaborative spirit of healing, underscoring the profound truth that while the journey may be complex, it need not be walked alone. The collective strength, understanding, and empathy found within these networks illuminate the path toward stability, recovery, and hope.

CHAPTER 3

The Patient's Perspective: Living with Bipolar Disorder

This chapter delves into the nuanced realities faced by individuals navigating this complex condition. It offers an intimate glimpse into the daily challenges and triumphs that define living with bipolar disorder, from the unpredictability of mood swings to the profound moments of personal achievement.

Exploring key aspects of self-management, such as mood and trigger tracking, alongside strategies for building resilience through coping mechanisms and mindfulness, this chapter equips readers with practical tools for empowerment. It underscores the importance of effective communication with healthcare providers and advocates for a shift in perspective—moving beyond the stigma to embrace one's identity and capabilities.

Daily Life with Bipolar Disorder

Embarking on a journey with bipolar disorder is to navigate a path fraught with challenges that test one's resilience, sense of self, and aspirations, yet it's also a journey marked by remarkable victories and personal growth. This condition profoundly influences every aspect of an individual's life, from the deeply introspective battles with self-identity to the external challenges of maintaining relationships and achieving professional success. However, within this intricate web of struggles, there are moments of triumph and resilience that shine brightly, offering hope and a testament to the human spirit's capacity to overcome adversity.

The oscillation between manic and depressive states in bipolar disorder necessitates a continuous exploration and re-evaluation of one's identity. This journey of self-discovery is vividly illustrated in the life of Marcus, a software developer whose manic phases spark bursts of extraordinary productivity and creativity. Initially, Marcus viewed these periods as the pinnacle of his abilities, only to grapple with feelings of inadequacy and loss of identity during the depressive downturns. Through sustained therapy and introspection, Marcus began to recognize his intrinsic worth beyond his bipolar episodes, embracing a more holistic view of his identity that encompasses his passion for coding, love for music, and his struggles and victories over bipolar disorder. This acknowledgment of his multifaceted identity represents a significant victory— breaking free from the shadow of bipolar disorder to celebrate the entirety of his being.

Relationship dynamics often undergo significant strain for individuals managing bipolar disorder, with the unpredictability of mood episodes posing a challenge to maintaining stable and supportive connections. Anna's story sheds light on this struggle. Her journey through bipolar disorder strained many friendships, as not everyone understood her sudden mood changes or need for isolation. However, it was through these challenges that Anna and her remaining friends forged deeper, more meaningful bonds. They established a mutual understanding and communication strategy that allowed Anna to express her needs without fear of judgment, and in turn, her friends learned how to offer support in truly helpful ways. This transformation in her social relationships underscores a vital triumph—the realization that while bipolar disorder may redefine relationships, it can also deepen them, cultivating a support network characterized by empathy, strength, and unconditional support.

In the professional realm, navigating bipolar disorder presents its own set of hurdles, as maintaining consistency and managing symptoms within the workplace can be daunting. The narrative of Laura, a high school teacher, exemplifies resilience in this aspect. Faced with the challenge of managing depressive episodes while meeting the demands of her teaching role, Laura initially feared her career was unsustainable. However, by implementing a comprehensive self-care routine, including regular therapy sessions, medication management, and open communication with her school administration about her needs, Laura not only excelled in her role but also became an advocate for mental health awareness among her colleagues and students. Her journey from fearing professional inadequacy to becoming a beacon of strength and awareness in her community highlights the triumphs possible when navigating bipolar disorder with courage and support.

Furthermore, the realm of personal hobbies and social interactions provides a canvas for individuals with bipolar disorder to paint experiences of joy, achievement, and normalcy against the backdrop of their condition. John, an amateur photographer, found in his passion for photography a therapeutic outlet and a means of connection. Through his lens, John captures moments of beauty that serve as reminders of stability during times of turmoil. His photography not only offers him personal solace but has also opened doors to social interactions and exhibitions, where he shares his journey and the role of photography in his management of bipolar disorder. John's story is a testament to how personal interests can become powerful tools in the journey toward resilience, offering a sense of purpose and fulfillment that transcends the challenges of living with bipolar disorder.

These narratives offer a rich, layered perspective on the daily realities of managing bipolar disorder, emphasizing the relentless negotiation between health management and the pursuit of personal and professional fulfillment. They celebrate the capacity for resilience, growth, and fulfillment that individuals with bipolar disorder harness as they navigate their condition. Through their stories of overcoming obstacles, developing strong coping skills, and building meaningful lives, a vivid picture emerges—one that honors the complexity of bipolar disorder while spotlighting the triumphs and victories that define the journey.

Self-Management Strategies

Effective self-management in bipolar disorder transcends basic care; it requires an in-depth understanding of one's emotional patterns, triggers, and the nuanced interplay between lifestyle and mood stability. This meticulous process is foundational for individuals seeking to navigate the complexities of their condition with autonomy and insight. At the heart of self-management is mood tracking—a systematic approach to observing and recording one's emotional states, triggers, and the outcomes of various treatment strategies.

This practice, whether executed through traditional pen-and-paper methods or leveraged via advanced digital tools, serves as a critical mechanism for identifying the precursors and patterns of mood episodes, thus empowering individuals with the knowledge to preemptively address potential swings. The traditional pen-and-paper mood diary offers a tangible, introspective medium for individuals to chronicle their daily emotional states, significant life events, medication adherence, and sleep quality. This method encourages a routine of reflection, enabling individuals to detect correlations between specific activities, stressors, and their mood fluctuations over time.

The act of writing itself can be therapeutic, providing a space for individuals to express their feelings and concerns in a concrete format. Conversely, digital platforms and applications for mood tracking present a dynamic and interactive alternative, equipped with functionalities that can analyze mood trends, visualize data through graphs, and even facilitate the sharing of this information with healthcare providers. These digital tools often incorporate reminders for medication and appointments, making them invaluable for individuals seeking a comprehensive and integrative approach to managing their bipolar disorder.

Beyond the identification of mood patterns and triggers, effective self-management also encompasses strategies for mitigating the impact of these identified stressors. Tailoring one's lifestyle to minimize known triggers is essential; this might involve adopting stress-reduction techniques such as yoga, deep breathing exercises, or engaging in regular physical activities known to bolster mental health. For some, addressing sleep disturbances through rigorous sleep hygiene practices or navigating social interactions to avoid stress-inducing scenarios can significantly reduce the likelihood of mood episode triggers.

Creating a personalized wellness plan is an extension of these management strategies, encapsulating a holistic view of self-care that balances physical health, mental well-being, and emotional resilience. This plan is comprehensive, addressing diet—emphasizing the consumption of mood-stabilizing nutrients and foods—physical exercise, and engagement in activities that foster a sense of achievement and happiness. Moreover, developing coping strategies tailored to individual experiences becomes crucial. These strategies may include techniques learned in cognitive-behavioral therapy, support from peer groups, or personal practices that have historically provided relief during challenging periods.

Empowering individuals with bipolar disorder to take an active role in their care through detailed mood tracking and strategic trigger management does more than equip them with tools for episode prevention; it fosters a profound connection to their mental health journey. This approach not only aids in preempting potential mood fluctuations but also cultivates a comprehensive skill set that supports overall wellness and stability. By engaging in this vigilant process of self-monitoring and response planning, individuals gain invaluable insights into their condition, enabling them to make informed decisions about their care and lifestyle adjustments.

This extensive guide to recognizing mood patterns, managing triggers, and adopting a personalized wellness strategy underscores the essence of self-management in bipolar disorder: it is a practice of constant engagement, learning, and adaptation. By rigorously implementing these strategies, individuals living with bipolar disorder can attain enhanced control over their symptoms, resulting in a better quality of life and greater satisfaction.

Building Resilience

Building resilience in the face of bipolar disorder is a journey of harnessing a diverse set of skills and practices that bolster one's ability to navigate the complexities of the condition. This intricate process involves emotional regulation, psychological fortitude, and the nurturing of supportive social networks, each contributing to a holistic approach to resilience. Below, we delve into these aspects in greater detail, offering insights and practical strategies for individuals seeking to fortify their resilience against the challenges posed by bipolar disorder.

Emotional Regulation through Mindfulness and Meditation

Emotional regulation is a cornerstone in managing the turbulent waves of bipolar disorder, with mindfulness and meditation serving as key practices in this endeavor. These techniques anchor individuals in the present moment, creating a buffer against the overwhelming emotions that can lead to mood episodes. Mindfulness, which involves staying aware of our thoughts, emotions, physical sensations, and the environment around us from one moment to the next, has demonstrated considerable potential in improving the management of emotions in individuals with bipolar disorder. It teaches individuals to observe their emotional states without judgment, fostering a sense of calm and acceptance.

Meditation, particularly mindfulness meditation, further supports this by encouraging a deep state of relaxation and focus. Studies have highlighted how regular mindfulness practice can reduce the severity of depressive and manic symptoms, largely by mitigating stress and promoting a balanced emotional state. This practice not only aids in managing the immediate symptoms of bipolar disorder but also contributes to long-term emotional well-being, helping individuals develop a more harmonious relationship with their internal emotional landscape.

Implementing mindfulness and meditation into daily life can significantly enhance an individual's ability to regulate their emotions effectively. Starting with simple practices such as focused breathing exercises for a few minutes each day can lay the groundwork for a more comprehensive mindfulness routine. This can gradually evolve into longer meditation sessions, incorporating practices like body scans, mindful walking, or guided meditations. The flexibility of mindfulness and meditation means they can be adapted to fit any lifestyle, with numerous resources available online to guide beginners.

By dedicating time each day to these practices, individuals with bipolar disorder can cultivate a space of mental clarity and calm, providing them with the tools to navigate their emotions more skillfully. This proactive approach to emotional regulation through mindfulness and meditation is a testament to the power of these practices in building resilience and empowering those with bipolar disorder to face their condition with strength and grace.

Psychological Coping Mechanisms

Psychological coping mechanisms are indispensable tools in the resilience-building toolkit for individuals navigating the complexities of bipolar disorder. These mechanisms encompass a range of strategies and skills designed to manage the mental and emotional aspects of the condition, enabling individuals to confront and adapt to the challenges it presents. Cognitive-behavioral techniques, such as cognitive restructuring, play a pivotal role in this context by helping individuals identify, challenge, and modify negative thought patterns that can exacerbate mood episodes.

By learning to reframe these thoughts into more balanced and positive narratives, individuals can significantly reduce the impact of stressors that trigger depressive or manic episodes. Moreover, problem-solving skills are enhanced through these psychological practices, empowering individuals to tackle challenges with a clear, structured approach that mitigates feelings of overwhelm and helplessness. Developing these skills not only aids in managing the immediate symptoms of bipolar disorder but also contributes to a foundation of psychological resilience that supports long-term mental health and stability.

Beyond cognitive strategies, creative expression emerges as a therapeutic and enriching psychological coping mechanism for many dealing with bipolar disorder. Whether through art, writing, music, or another form of creative outlet, engaging in creative activities provides a means of expressing emotions, processing experiences, and finding a sense of accomplishment and identity outside the disorder. This creative process can offer a cathartic release for pent-up emotions, serving as a safe and constructive way to navigate the emotional highs and lows characteristic of bipolar disorder.

Additionally, physical activity is recognized for its mental health benefits, including the reduction of anxiety and depressive symptoms and the improvement of mood and self-esteem. Incorporating regular physical exercise into one's routine can act as a powerful psychological coping mechanism, leveraging the body's natural stress-reducing chemicals to foster a sense of well-being. Collectively, these psychological coping mechanisms—cognitive restructuring, creative expression, and physical activity—form a multifaceted approach to building resilience, offering individuals with bipolar disorder valuable strategies for enhancing their mental health and navigating their condition with confidence and agency.

Building Social Resilience

Building social resilience is a critical aspect of managing bipolar disorder, emphasizing the importance of cultivating strong, supportive relationships and community connections. Social resilience refers to the ability to foster, maintain, and draw on these relationships during times of need, creating a network of support that can offer emotional comfort, practical assistance, and a sense of belonging. For individuals with bipolar disorder, this means actively engaging with family, friends, and support groups who understand the challenges of the condition and can provide non-judgmental support.

Establishing and nurturing these connections requires open communication about one's experiences with bipolar disorder, educating loved ones about the condition, and expressing clear needs and boundaries. In doing so, individuals can create a supportive environment that not only aids in managing day-to-day challenges but also enhances their capacity to withstand and recover from crises. Support groups, whether in-person or online, play a pivotal role in social resilience, offering a platform to share experiences, coping strategies, and mutual encouragement with others who understand the intricacies of living with bipolar disorder.

Moreover, building social resilience goes beyond receiving support; it involves contributing to the well-being of others and fostering a reciprocal relationship of care and support within one's network. This exchange enhances the individual's sense of purpose and self-worth, further solidifying their social resilience. For caregivers and family members, part of building social resilience includes prioritizing their well-being, and recognizing that they can better support their loved one if they are also supported.

This may involve seeking their support networks, engaging in self-care practices, and setting healthy boundaries to prevent caregiver burnout. Ultimately, social resilience for those with bipolar disorder is about creating a balanced ecosystem of giving and receiving support, characterized by empathy, understanding, and shared growth. Through the cultivation of these robust social networks, individuals with bipolar disorder can experience a deeper sense of community and resilience, empowering them to navigate their condition with greater confidence and stability.

Implementing Resilience Strategies

Implementing resilience strategies in the management of bipolar disorder is a multifaceted process that requires consistency, awareness, and a proactive approach. It involves integrating coping mechanisms and mindfulness practices into daily life, forming a comprehensive regimen that addresses the condition's emotional, psychological, and social dimensions. The first step in this implementation process is the cultivation of self-awareness—recognizing the signs of mood fluctuations and understanding personal triggers that may precipitate episodes.

This awareness allows individuals to employ specific resilience strategies, such as engaging in mindfulness meditation during times of stress or utilizing cognitive-behavioral techniques to challenge negative thought patterns. By setting aside dedicated time for these practices, whether it's a few minutes of mindfulness each morning or scheduled sessions for cognitive restructuring exercises, individuals can develop a routine that fosters emotional regulation and psychological strength.

Moreover, the successful implementation of resilience strategies extends beyond individual practices to include the development of a supportive social network. This involves communicating openly with family, friends, and healthcare providers about one's needs and effective strategies for support. Education plays a crucial role here, as informed supporters are better equipped to provide meaningful assistance. Additionally, individuals are encouraged to seek out and participate in support groups or communities, where shared experiences and strategies can offer further insight and reinforcement of coping mechanisms.

Implementing resilience strategies is an ongoing journey of adaptation and growth, requiring flexibility to adjust practices as one's needs and circumstances evolve. By actively engaging in this process, individuals with bipolar disorder can enhance their capacity to navigate the condition with resilience, leading to improved well-being and a more fulfilling life.

Through exploration of these strategies and the incorporation of practical advice, this section aims to empower individuals with bipolar disorder to build a robust set of tools for navigating their emotional landscape with resilience and grace. By facing adversity with knowledge, support, and proactive self-management, individuals can aspire to a life marked by stability, fulfillment, and personal growth.

Advocating for Yourself

Self-advocacy in managing bipolar disorder is paramount, empowering individuals to navigate their healthcare journey with confidence and clarity. Effective communication with healthcare providers is not just beneficial—it's essential for ensuring that treatment plans are tailored to meet the unique needs of each individual. Assertively articulating one's experiences, preferences, and concerns lays the foundation for a collaborative and productive relationship with care providers, one where decisions are made jointly, respecting the patient's autonomy and informed consent.

Strategies for Effective Communication

The cornerstone of self-advocacy is the ability to communicate openly and effectively with healthcare professionals. This involves being clear and assertive when discussing symptoms, treatment effects, and personal goals for managing the disorder. Maintaining a healthcare journal can be incredibly beneficial in this regard. By documenting daily mood variations, medication side effects, triggers, and overall well-being, individuals create a comprehensive record that can inform discussions with their healthcare team.

Preparing questions and talking points in advance of appointments ensures that key concerns are addressed, and nothing is overlooked in the conversation. Additionally, bringing a trusted friend or family member to appointments can provide emotional support and help in remembering the discussion details or advocating on the patient's behalf if needed.

Navigating the Healthcare Team and Understanding Patient Rights

Managing a healthcare team effectively requires understanding the roles of various professionals involved in bipolar disorder treatment—from psychiatrists and psychologists to primary care physicians and pharmacists. It's important for individuals to know that they have the right to seek second opinions, ask for explanations about treatment options, and be fully informed about the risks and benefits of proposed therapies. Informed consent is a fundamental patient right, ensuring that individuals are active participants in their care decisions rather than passive recipients of medical advice. Knowing one's rights in the medical decision-making process fosters a sense of empowerment and engagement, crucial for a positive healthcare experience.

Practical Tips for a Proactive Healthcare Experience

- **Healthcare Journal**: Keeping an up-to-date record of all aspects of one's health and treatment can dramatically improve the quality of care received. This journal acts as a vital tool for tracking progress, understanding triggers, and evaluating the effectiveness of treatment strategies.

- **Appointment Preparation**: Writing down all questions and observations before healthcare visits can help maximize the value of each appointment. It ensures that no critical issue is overlooked and facilitates a focused, productive discussion with healthcare providers.

- **Educational Empowerment**: Acquiring a deep understanding of bipolar disorder and the latest treatment options enables patients to engage in more meaningful conversations with their healthcare team. Knowledge is power, and in the context of healthcare, it equips individuals with the ability to make informed decisions about their treatment.

- **Supportive Attendance**: Having a reliable support person during appointments can provide emotional reassurance and ensure that all information is accurately communicated and understood. This support can be invaluable in navigating complex healthcare information and decisions.

- **Clarification and Advocacy**: Never hesitate to ask for clarification if certain aspects of the treatment or medical terminology are unclear. Assertive communication and asking for detailed explanations are integral to informed decision-making and self-advocacy.

Empowering oneself to advocate effectively within the healthcare system is a crucial step toward managing bipolar disorder successfully. By employing strategies for effective communication, understanding how to navigate the healthcare team, and being proactive in healthcare encounters, individuals can ensure that their voices are heard and respected. This active engagement in the healthcare process fosters a partnership with care providers, based on mutual respect and collaboration, ultimately leading to a treatment plan that aligns with the patient's needs, preferences, and life goals.

Beyond Stigma: Embracing Your Identity and Capabilities

Tackling the pervasive stigma surrounding bipolar disorder requires a multifaceted approach, emphasizing not only the critique of societal misunderstandings but also the promotion of self-empowerment and broader societal change. The journey towards dismantling stigma and embracing personal identity beyond a diagnosis is both deeply personal and inherently collective, involving individual action, community support, and systemic advocacy to reshape perceptions of mental health.

Understanding and Addressing Stigma

Understanding and addressing the stigma associated with bipolar disorder is essential in the journey toward embracing one's identity and capabilities beyond the diagnosis. Stigma, deeply ingrained in societal attitudes and misconceptions about mental health, casts a shadow over individuals with bipolar disorder, often leading to prejudice, discrimination, and isolation. This stigma stems from a lack of knowledge, fear of the unknown, and pervasive myths that mischaracterize bipolar disorder as simply erratic behavior rather than a complex and manageable mental health condition.

It can deter individuals from seeking the help they need, hinder their opportunities for employment and social interaction, and contribute to an internalized sense of shame and inadequacy. Addressing this stigma requires a concerted effort to educate the public on the realities of bipolar disorder, emphasizing that it is a part of the individual's life, not the entirety of their identity. By challenging and changing the narrative around bipolar disorder through awareness campaigns, personal storytelling, and advocacy, society can move toward a more inclusive and understanding perspective.

Furthermore, confronting and dismantling internalized stigma is a critical step for individuals with bipolar disorder in reclaiming their sense of self-worth and agency. Internalized stigma occurs when individuals absorb and believe the negative stereotypes and prejudices held by society, leading to self-stigmatization and a diminished sense of self. Combatting this requires individuals to actively challenge these negative beliefs, recognize their intrinsic value, and affirm their strengths and accomplishments.

Practices such as engaging in positive self-talk, connecting with supportive communities who understand the bipolar experience, and celebrating personal successes can help mitigate the effects of internalized stigma. Empowerment comes from recognizing that while bipolar disorder is a part of one's life experience, it does not define one's identity or limit one's capabilities. Through understanding and actively addressing both external and internalized stigma, individuals with bipolar disorder can foster a stronger sense of self and embrace their full potential, contributing positively to changing societal perceptions of mental health.

Empowerment Through Self-Advocacy

Empowerment through self-advocacy is a transformative process for individuals with bipolar disorder, serving as a vital pathway to embracing their identity and realizing their full potential despite societal stigma. Self-advocacy involves taking an active role in one's healthcare journey, from accurately communicating symptoms and treatment effects to healthcare providers, to making informed decisions about care options. This proactive stance enables individuals to assert control over their treatment and challenge any disparities or misunderstandings within the healthcare system.

Moreover, self-advocacy extends beyond the clinical setting, encompassing the right to seek fulfilling opportunities in education, employment, and social engagements, advocating for accommodations when necessary. By developing the skills to effectively articulate their needs and rights, individuals with bipolar disorder can navigate the challenges of their condition with confidence, ensuring that their voices are heard and respected across all spheres of life.

Furthermore, empowerment through self-advocacy plays a crucial role in dismantling internalized stigma, encouraging individuals to recognize their intrinsic worth and capabilities. It prompts a shift in perspective, from viewing oneself through the lens of societal prejudice to acknowledging and celebrating one's identity beyond the diagnosis. This shift fosters resilience, self-respect, and a positive self-image, which are essential for personal growth and fulfillment. Engaging in self-advocacy also inspires others within the bipolar disorder community, creating a ripple effect of empowerment and challenging societal attitudes toward mental health.

Through shared experiences and collective advocacy, individuals can contribute to a more inclusive and understanding society where mental health is embraced as part of human diversity. Thus, empowerment through self-advocacy is not only about navigating the healthcare system and societal structures; it's about reclaiming one's narrative, affirming one's strengths, and advocating for a future where individuals with bipolar disorder are valued for their entire selves, not defined by their condition.

Celebrating Individuality and Strength

Celebrating individuality and strength is a crucial aspect of moving beyond the stigma associated with bipolar disorder. This celebration is about recognizing and embracing the unique qualities, talents, and experiences that define each person, rather than allowing a diagnosis to overshadow their identity. Individuals with bipolar disorder often possess profound resilience, creativity, and empathy—qualities that are honed through their experiences of navigating the highs and lows of the condition.

Acknowledging these strengths is essential not only for personal empowerment but also for challenging societal perceptions that tend to focus on the limitations of the disorder. By highlighting the accomplishments, talents, and contributions of individuals with bipolar disorder, the narrative shifts from one of stigma and limitation to one of diversity and potential. This recognition fosters a sense of pride and self-worth, empowering individuals to pursue their passions and goals with confidence, regardless of the challenges they face.

Moreover, celebrating individuality and strength involves creating spaces where the voices and stories of those with bipolar disorder are heard and valued. This can be achieved through community events, art exhibitions, writing, and speaking engagements that allow individuals to share their journeys, showcasing the rich tapestry of experiences that come with living with bipolar disorder. Such platforms not only serve to empower those sharing their stories but also educate the wider public, breaking down myths and building empathy. Encouraging this celebration of diversity and resilience helps to cultivate a more inclusive society, where mental health is understood as a part of human diversity rather than a marker of difference.

In embracing and championing their identity beyond bipolar disorder, individuals can inspire a cultural shift towards a future where everyone is recognized for their full selves, contributing to a world that appreciates the strength in diversity and the beauty in overcoming adversity.

The Role of Community and Visibility in Advocacy

The role of community and visibility in advocacy is pivotal in transcending the stigma associated with bipolar disorder and fostering a society that embraces mental health as an integral aspect of human diversity. Community, whether formed through support groups, online forums, or mental health organizations, provides a sanctuary for individuals to share their experiences, challenges, and triumphs related to living with bipolar disorder.

These spaces are not only crucial for offering support and understanding but also serve as platforms for collective advocacy. By uniting voices, individuals can amplify their message, advocating for increased awareness, better mental health resources, and policies that support those living with bipolar disorder. Visibility plays a complementary role in this advocacy effort. As individuals with bipolar disorder and their allies share their stories openly, they challenge stereotypes and demystify the condition. High-profile individuals coming forward with their experiences can particularly impact public perceptions, highlighting that bipolar disorder does not discriminate and that those affected can lead successful, fulfilling lives.

Together, community and visibility foster a sense of belonging and empowerment, driving forward the movement to normalize conversations about mental health and challenge societal stigma. Moreover, the intersection of community engagement and visibility in advocacy efforts has the transformative potential to reshape societal attitudes towards bipolar disorder and mental health more broadly. Through organized campaigns, awareness events, and participation in mental health discussions, individuals and communities can influence public opinion and policy, pushing for a future where mental health care is accessible, and stigma is eradicated.

Visibility in advocacy also extends to the digital realm, where social media and online platforms can reach wide audiences, spreading educational content and personal narratives that foster understanding and empathy. By highlighting the collective strength and resilience of the bipolar disorder community, these advocacy efforts contribute to a cultural shift towards inclusivity and acceptance. Emphasizing the value of community and the power of visibility, individuals can move beyond stigma, advocating for a world that recognizes and celebrates the diversity and capabilities of people with bipolar disorder, paving the way for greater acceptance and support.

Envisioning a Stigma-Free Future

Envisioning a stigma-free future for individuals with bipolar disorder is an essential and hopeful aspect of moving beyond current societal misconceptions and embracing a broader, more inclusive understanding of mental health. In this future, bipolar disorder and other mental health conditions are recognized as part of the rich tapestry of human experience, not as markers of difference to be shunned or feared. Achieving this vision requires a collective shift in perspective, from viewing mental health through a lens of fear and stigma to one of empathy, education, and acceptance.

It entails comprehensive mental health education that starts early, breaking down myths and fostering an environment where young people grow up understanding mental health as a key component of overall well-being. In a stigma-free future, conversations about mental health are as commonplace and destigmatized as those about physical health, and individuals feel empowered to seek help without the fear of judgment or discrimination. This paradigm shift also involves media representation that accurately and sensitively portrays bipolar disorder, contributing to public understanding and empathy.

Moreover, a stigma-free future is built on the foundations of robust support systems and accessible, high-quality mental health services for all. In this envisioned future, healthcare systems are equipped to offer comprehensive, personalized care that addresses the unique needs of each individual with bipolar disorder, ensuring that no one is left to navigate their condition in isolation. Legal and workplace protections for individuals with mental health conditions are firmly in place, ensuring that they can pursue their careers and goals without facing discrimination.

Advocacy and visibility continue to play crucial roles, with individuals and communities sharing their stories and experiences to challenge lingering prejudices and build a more accepting society. Ultimately, envisioning a stigma-free future is not just about eradicating negative perceptions of bipolar disorder; it's about creating a world where every individual is valued for their whole self, where mental health is embraced as a vital aspect of diversity, and where everyone has the opportunity to live a fulfilling life, irrespective of their mental health status.

In conclusion, moving beyond stigma towards a place of empowerment and acceptance for those living with bipolar disorder is a journey that demands persistence, courage, and collective action. By embracing their identities, advocating for their needs, and fostering communities of support, individuals can challenge societal perceptions and contribute to a more inclusive, empathetic world.

CHAPTER 4

The Support Network's Guide

This chapter illuminates the pivotal role of the support network in providing effective, empathetic assistance that genuinely benefits those living with bipolar disorder. It delves into the essence of meaningful support, highlighting the importance of understanding the complexities of the condition and offering guidance tailored to enhance the well-being of both the individual and their supporters.

Expanding further, the chapter explores practical communication strategies for discussing bipolar disorder, fostering an environment where open, honest dialogue flourishes. It addresses the critical need for caregivers to maintain their well-being through setting boundaries and practicing self-care, ensuring they remain resilient and capable of providing support.

Understanding Your Role: How to Offer Help That Helps

Understanding the multifaceted role of caregivers and support networks in the lives of those with bipolar disorder is essential for providing effective and empowering assistance. The journey of supporting someone with bipolar disorder involves more than simply being physically present; it requires a deep understanding of the disorder, a respect for the individual's autonomy, and a commitment to offering support that genuinely enhances their well-being. Educating oneself about the complexities and unpredictabilities of bipolar disorder is the first crucial step. Knowledge about the disorder's symptoms, treatment options, and potential challenges enables caregivers to offer informed support, anticipate needs, and understand the individual's experiences more deeply.

The concept of "help that helps" underscores the importance of providing support that empowers the individual with bipolar disorder to maintain control over their life and treatment decisions. This type of support can be categorized into emotional, practical, and informational roles, each playing a critical part in the caregiver's repertoire. Emotional support involves offering empathy, understanding, and encouragement, creating a safe space where feelings and experiences can be shared without judgment.

Practical support may include assisting with daily tasks, accompanying the individual to appointments, or helping manage medication schedules, thereby reducing stress and promoting treatment adherence. Informational support involves sharing researched information about bipolar disorder, treatment options, and resources, empowering the individual to make informed decisions about their care.

However, offering "help that helps" also involves respecting the independence and autonomy of the individual with bipolar disorder. It's about striking a delicate balance between providing necessary support and empowering them to lead their treatment and management of the condition. This balance requires open communication, where the preferences, needs, and boundaries of the individual are discussed and respected. Caregivers must be attentive to the signals that indicate when their involvement is needed and when stepping back is more beneficial, allowing the person with bipolar disorder to navigate their journey with a sense of ownership and self-efficacy.

Special emphasis must also be placed on the caregiver's approach to offering help. Actions and support should be offered in a way that empowers the individual, rather than creating dependency or infringing on their sense of control. This might involve collaborative problem-solving, where caregivers and their loved ones work together to identify challenges and solutions, fostering a partnership rather than a dependency. Additionally, recognizing and celebrating the achievements and progress of individuals with bipolar disorder reinforces their capabilities and strengths, further empowering them in their journey.

Ultimately, understanding your role as a caregiver or member of a support network means embracing the complexity of bipolar disorder and recognizing the unique needs and preferences of your loved one. It's about offering support that is both respectful and empowering, facilitating a journey towards wellness that is collaborative and respectful. By adopting a nuanced approach to caregiving—grounded in education, empathy, and empowerment—caregivers can ensure that their support is genuinely beneficial, contributing positively to the lives of those with bipolar disorder and reinforcing their ability to navigate the condition with confidence and autonomy.

Communication Strategies

Navigating conversations about bipolar disorder demands sensitivity, understanding, and a commitment to open, honest dialogue. Effective communication is foundational for building trust, offering support, and fostering mutual understanding between individuals with bipolar disorder and their caregivers. It can be challenging to discuss topics such as seeking help, treatment options, and behaviors symptomatic of the disorder, yet these conversations are essential for ensuring that individuals feel supported and understood. This section delves into strategies designed to facilitate meaningful discussions, aiming to strengthen the communicative bond between caregivers and their loved ones.

Approaching Sensitive Topics

Approaching sensitive topics within the context of bipolar disorder requires a careful, empathetic approach that respects the feelings and autonomy of the individual. Initiating conversations about seeking help, considering treatment options, or discussing behaviors symptomatic of the disorder is inherently challenging, given the potential for these discussions to evoke feelings of vulnerability or defensiveness. Caregivers and support networks must frame these conversations in a manner that emphasizes care, concern, and a shared goal of well-being.

Prefacing discussions with affirmations of support and understanding can help set a positive tone. For instance, beginning with statements like, "I truly care about your happiness and health," can signal good intentions. It's also beneficial to choose a calm, comfortable environment for these discussions, where distractions are minimized, and privacy is ensured, making it easier for the individual to open up and engage in dialogue.

Moreover, when delving into these sensitive areas, it's imperative to use language that avoids implications of blame or judgment. Focusing on specific observations and expressing concern in a non-accusatory manner can foster a more receptive environment. For instance, saying, "I've observed that you've had quite a few highs and lows recently, and it appears to have been quite challenging for you." How are you feeling about it?" offers an invitation for open communication rather than an indictment. This approach allows caregivers to express their concerns and observations while giving the individual space to share their perspectives.

Active listening plays a crucial role here, as does the willingness to acknowledge the individual's feelings and experiences. By approaching sensitive topics with empathy, patience, and a focus on collaboration, caregivers can encourage meaningful dialogue that reinforces the support system's role as a source of unwavering support and understanding.

Active Listening and Validation

Active listening and validation are cornerstone communication strategies for support networks engaging with individuals who have bipolar disorder. Active listening goes beyond merely hearing words; it involves fully engaging with and understanding the speaker's message. This means giving undivided attention, observing non-verbal cues, and reflecting on what has been said to ensure comprehension and empathy.

For caregivers and support networks, practicing active listening can dramatically improve communication with their loved ones. It signals respect for their feelings and perspectives, making it more likely for open and honest dialogue to flourish. Techniques such as nodding, maintaining eye contact, and using verbal affirmations like "I see" or "That sounds challenging" reinforce that the speaker's experiences are being taken seriously. This level of engagement helps to break down barriers, encouraging individuals with bipolar disorder to share more freely, secure in the knowledge that their support system is truly listening and seeking to understand their experiences.

Validation, a critical component of active listening, involves recognizing and accepting another person's feelings and experiences as valid and significant, regardless of one's viewpoint. In conversations about bipolar disorder, validation can be particularly powerful. It reassures the individual that their emotions and experiences are legitimate and deserving of attention. This doesn't mean agreeing with everything they say but acknowledging their feelings and experiences without judgment.

Phrases like "It's understandable you feel that way given what you've been through" or "Your feelings are completely valid" can make a profound difference in how supported and understood someone feels. Validation can mitigate feelings of isolation and foster a supportive atmosphere where challenging topics are more easily navigated. Together, active listening and validation not only enhance communication but also strengthen the bond between individuals with bipolar disorder and their support networks, laying a foundation for more effective support and mutual trust.

Non-Confrontational Language

Utilizing non-confrontational language is an essential strategy in effectively communicating with someone living with bipolar disorder. This approach involves choosing words and phrases that minimize the potential for the listener to feel blamed, judged, or attacked, thereby reducing the likelihood of defensive responses. Non-confrontational communication is about framing observations, concerns, and suggestions in a way that conveys support and understanding, rather than criticism.

For example, expressing concern by saying, "I've noticed some changes in your behavior that worry me, and I'm here to support you," is far more constructive than accusatory statements that might begin with "You always..." or "You never..." Such language encourages a more open and productive dialogue by focusing on the issue at hand rather than assigning blame. It's a way of speaking that fosters trust and cooperation, inviting the individual with bipolar disorder to engage in a conversation about their experiences and needs without fear of reprisal or misunderstanding.

Moreover, non-confrontational language includes actively avoiding terms that stigmatize mental health conditions, instead choosing words that reflect a compassionate understanding of bipolar disorder as a medical condition. Phrases that validate the individual's feelings and experiences, while also gently encouraging them to consider their impact, are particularly effective. For instance, saying, "It sounds like you're having a tough time right now. How can I help?" provides space for the individual to articulate their needs and preferences.

This communication style also extends to discussing treatment options and lifestyle adjustments, where collaborative language can be used to explore possibilities together, such as, "What do you think about trying this new approach to see if it helps?" Through the regular use of non-confrontational language, caregivers and support networks can create an atmosphere of communication characterized by empathy, respect, and mutual comprehension, laying the foundation for significant support and connection.

Breaking Down Barriers to Communication

Breaking down communication barriers is crucial in nurturing a supportive and understanding relationship with individuals living with bipolar disorder. These barriers often stem from misconceptions about the disorder, fear of saying the wrong thing, or discomfort in discussing mental health issues. Overcoming these obstacles requires a deliberate and compassionate approach, beginning with education and a willingness to learn about bipolar disorder from both medical and personal perspectives.

By gaining a deeper understanding of the condition, its symptoms, and the individual experiences of those affected, caregivers and support networks can approach conversations with empathy and insight. Educating oneself not only dispels myths and reduces personal discomfort but also signals to the individual with bipolar disorder that their support system is genuinely interested in understanding their experience. This foundation of knowledge and empathy is key to establishing trust, which is essential for open and honest communication.

Furthermore, creating an environment where mental health can be discussed openly and without judgment is another critical step in breaking down communication barriers. This involves actively challenging societal stigma surrounding mental health and modeling positive communication behaviors, such as using respectful language, listening actively, and validating feelings. Encouraging regular, informal conversations about mental health can normalize these discussions, making it easier to talk about more challenging topics as they arise.

It's also important for caregivers to share their feelings and experiences, as appropriate, to further democratize the conversation around mental health. Demonstrating vulnerability can strengthen the bond between caregivers and those with bipolar disorder, emphasizing that mental health is a shared human experience. By addressing these barriers to communication with education, empathy, and openness, caregivers can foster a supportive dialogue that enhances the well-being of individuals with bipolar disorder, promoting a relationship based on mutual understanding and respect.

Setting Boundaries: Self-Care for Caregivers

Establishing boundaries is a critical component of self-care for caregivers, particularly those supporting individuals with bipolar disorder. It's a nuanced process that requires an understanding of one's limits and the ability to communicate these boundaries effectively. The essence of setting boundaries lies in the acknowledgment that while caregivers are committed to supporting their loved ones, they also need to protect their mental, emotional, and physical health. This dual focus ensures that caregivers can provide support in a healthy, sustainable manner, preventing caregiver fatigue and burnout.

For instance, caregivers might set boundaries around their availability, specifying times when they are and aren't able to provide support or delineate the types of support they can offer. This clarity helps manage expectations and fosters a supportive environment that respects the needs of both the caregiver and the individual with bipolar disorder. Recognizing the signs of caregiver fatigue is paramount in this balancing act. Symptoms such as persistent exhaustion, feelings of irritability, a sense of being overwhelmed, and neglecting one's own needs and interests are red flags signaling that boundaries may need to be reassessed. Caregivers must heed these signs and implement self-care strategies proactively.

Self-care might encompass scheduling regular periods for rest and activities that rejuvenate the spirit, such as pursuing hobbies, engaging in physical exercise, or simply enjoying moments of solitude. Maintaining social connections outside the caregiving role is equally important, offering caregivers a network of support and understanding, which is vital for their emotional well-being. These connections provide a space for sharing experiences, exchanging advice, and receiving emotional support, which can bolster a caregiver's resilience and capacity to cope with the challenges of their role.

Moreover, effective communication about boundaries involves expressing needs and limitations with kindness and assertiveness, ensuring that the individual with bipolar disorder understands the caregiver's position without feeling abandoned or marginalized. Caregivers can benefit from practicing phrases that convey their boundaries respectfully, such as "I need to take some time for myself this evening, but let's talk about this more tomorrow," or "I'm not able to help with that, but let's find another solution together." It's about creating a dialogue that respects both the caregiver's well-being and the individual's needs, promoting a collaborative approach to managing bipolar disorder.

In reinforcing the concept that caregiving does not equate to self-sacrifice, this detailed exploration aims to empower caregivers with the tools and understanding necessary to care for themselves while supporting their loved ones. By emphasizing the importance of boundary-setting, recognizing signs of fatigue, and adopting comprehensive self-care practices, caregivers are better positioned to maintain their health and continue offering effective support.

Ultimately, the well-being of caregivers is intrinsically linked to their capacity to provide care, highlighting the necessity of self-care in the caregiving journey. Through careful attention to their own needs and proactive management of their responsibilities, caregivers can achieve a balanced and fulfilling role in the lives of those they support.

Supporting Treatment and Management Plans

Supporting a loved one through their treatment and management plan for bipolar disorder involves a commitment to understanding the condition, actively participating in the care process, and fostering an environment conducive to stability and wellness. Caregivers play a crucial role in this journey, offering practical support that can significantly impact the effectiveness of treatment strategies.

Assisting with Medication Management

Assisting with medication management for someone with bipolar disorder is a critical role that caregivers play, requiring diligence, organization, and open communication. This task goes beyond merely reminding the individual to take their medication; it encompasses understanding the purpose and potential side effects of each medication, as well as monitoring the overall effectiveness of the treatment plan. Caregivers can support medication management by establishing a routine for medication intake that aligns with the individual's daily schedule, using tools such as pill organizers and reminder alarms to ensure consistency.

Additionally, maintaining a detailed log that tracks medication doses, times of administration, and any side effects observed is invaluable. This log not only helps in identifying patterns that may indicate the need for dosage adjustments or medication changes but also provides concrete data that can be discussed with healthcare providers, ensuring that the treatment plan remains aligned with the individual's needs.

Moreover, engaging in discussions about medications with the individual is essential for fostering a sense of partnership and mutual understanding in the management of bipolar disorder. This involves encouraging open dialogue about how the medications make them feel, any concerns they may have about side effects and their perceptions of the medication's impact on their symptoms. Caregivers should also advocate for their loved one during appointments with healthcare professionals, armed with the information from the medication log and any observations they have made.

By doing so, caregivers can help ensure that medication decisions are made collaboratively, taking into account the individual's experiences and preferences. Effective medication management is a cornerstone of successful bipolar disorder treatment, and through careful monitoring, organization, and communication, caregivers can significantly contribute to their loved one's well-being and stability.

Attending Appointments and Implementing Lifestyle Changes

Attending appointments with healthcare providers alongside a loved one with bipolar disorder is a significant aspect of support that caregivers can offer. This active involvement not only ensures that the individual is not alone in navigating their treatment but also allows caregivers to gain a deeper understanding of the condition, the treatment plan, and any adjustments that may be necessary over time. During these appointments, caregivers can serve as an additional set of ears, helping to recall important information discussed and asking clarifying questions that the individual might not think of or feel comfortable asking.

Moreover, caregivers can share their observations about their loved one's condition, providing valuable insights that might influence treatment decisions. By taking notes during appointments and discussing them afterward with their loved ones, caregivers help ensure that both they and the individual fully understand the treatment plan and any next steps, including changes in medication, therapy sessions, or lifestyle recommendations. Implementing lifestyle changes is another critical area where caregivers can provide substantial support.

Lifestyle adjustments, such as maintaining a regular sleep schedule, engaging in regular physical activity, and following a nutritious diet, can significantly impact the management of bipolar disorder. Caregivers can assist in these areas by helping to create a structured daily routine that incorporates these elements, offering encouragement and motivation to stick with these changes, and even participating alongside their loved ones to make these activities more enjoyable and sustainable.

For instance, planning and preparing healthy meals together can make dietary changes more manageable, while setting shared fitness goals or engaging in outdoor activities can make exercise a fun part of the daily routine. These lifestyle changes, while sometimes challenging to implement and maintain, play a crucial role in stabilizing mood and improving overall well-being for individuals with bipolar disorder. Caregivers, through their support, encouragement, and participation, can make a significant difference in the effectiveness of these lifestyle interventions, enhancing the quality of life and stability for their loved ones.

Preparing for Crisis Situations and Navigating the Healthcare System

Preparing for crisis situations when supporting a loved one with bipolar disorder involves creating a comprehensive plan that addresses potential emergencies, ensuring that both caregivers and individuals are equipped to handle sudden escalations or severe episodes effectively. This plan should include detailed information such as emergency contact numbers, including those of healthcare providers, local mental health services, and crisis hotlines. Additionally, a list of medications currently being taken, any known allergies, and a brief medical history should be readily accessible.

Caregivers should also familiarize themselves with the legal documents pertinent to healthcare decisions, such as advance directives or power of attorney, to make informed decisions on behalf of their loved one if necessary. Discussing and agreeing upon this crisis plan in advance with the individual and healthcare providers ensures that everyone involved understands the steps to take during an emergency, minimizing confusion and enabling a swift, coordinated response that prioritizes the individual's safety and health.

Navigating the healthcare system is another critical aspect of supporting someone with bipolar disorder, requiring caregivers to advocate for their loved one's needs while ensuring that they receive appropriate and timely care. This involves understanding the intricacies of insurance coverage, including what treatments and services are covered, and being aware of the rights and protections afforded to individuals with mental health conditions. Caregivers should also cultivate relationships with their loved one's healthcare team, acting as liaisons to communicate concerns, share observations, and obtain information.

Being proactive in managing appointments, seeking second opinions when necessary, and staying informed about the latest treatment options can empower caregivers to make informed decisions and advocate effectively. Moreover, caregivers can benefit from connecting with support groups and organizations dedicated to bipolar disorder, where they can access resources, guidance, and support from others who have navigated similar challenges. Through careful preparation for crisis situations and savvy navigation of the healthcare system, caregivers can play a pivotal role in managing their loved one's bipolar disorder, ensuring they have access to the care and support they need to manage their condition successfully.

By actively participating in their loved one's treatment and management plan for bipolar disorder, caregivers can make a substantial difference in the effectiveness of care. This support ranges from practical assistance with daily tasks to emotional support and advocacy, all aimed at promoting stability, wellness, and a fulfilling life.

Nurturing Relationships: Dealing with Strain and Strengthening Bonds

Navigating the intricacies of relationships affected by bipolar disorder demands an unwavering commitment to effective communication, which serves as the cornerstone for understanding and support. Achieving this level of communication necessitates the establishment of a safe and open environment where individual with bipolar disorder feels secure in sharing their experiences, emotions, and needs. Such an environment is fostered through the practice of active listening—where attention is fully given, and responses are crafted to reflect understanding and empathy.

Caregivers can enhance this environment by using strategies like paraphrasing what has been shared to ensure accurate comprehension and posing open-ended questions that encourage a deeper exploration of feelings and thoughts. The use of non-confrontational language, particularly through "I" statements, allows caregivers to express concerns and observations in a manner that minimizes the likelihood of defensiveness, fostering a dialogue based on mutual respect and shared objectives. This approach underlines the necessity of a communication channel that remains open and accessible, signaling to the person with bipolar disorder that their perspectives are valued and respected.

Empathy and patience are indispensable in the toolkit of those supporting someone with bipolar disorder. Empathy involves a profound effort to understand the person's internal struggle with their condition, recognizing the immense courage it takes to navigate such a complex landscape. Patience becomes crucial as the journey through bipolar disorder is marked by its unpredictability, with progress being non-linear and prone to setbacks. For caregivers, practicing patience means avoiding comparisons and staying supportive, even when faced with the challenges of the condition's fluctuating nature. Demonstrating empathy and patience in interactions—not only through words but also through actions and demeanor—can significantly alleviate the individual's sense of isolation, reinforcing the support system's role as a pillar of understanding and encouragement.

The role of shared experiences in fortifying the bonds between individuals with bipolar disorder and their supporters cannot be overstated. Participating in activities that both enjoy, from engaging in physical exercise to undertaking creative endeavors, offers precious moments of connection that transcend the confines of the disorder. It is in these moments that the relationship is strengthened and enriched, providing a counterbalance to the challenges posed by bipolar disorder. Furthermore, acknowledging and celebrating every instance of progress, no matter the scale, serves to highlight the effort and resilience of the individual, boosting their confidence and motivation. These celebrations and shared experiences lay the groundwork for a deeper, more meaningful connection, emphasizing the journey's value and the collective strength garnered through mutual support.

Self-care emerges as a critical aspect of maintaining a healthy and effective support network. For the individual with bipolar disorder, self-care may encompass a spectrum of practices from adhering to treatment protocols to engaging in activities that promote mental and physical well-being. For caregivers, self-care is equally essential; it ensures that they can provide sustained support without compromising their health. This might involve setting aside time for personal hobbies, seeking emotional support from peers, or recognizing when to seek professional help for themselves. Prioritizing self-care underscores the concept that one must be well to care well for others. It is a fundamental principle that sustains the capacity of caregivers to offer the support their loved ones need.

Through these practices, caregivers and individuals with bipolar disorder can navigate the condition's challenges together, reinforcing a support system characterized by understanding, resilience, and mutual respect. This enhanced dynamic not only facilitates better management of bipolar disorder but also contributes to the overall richness and depth of the relationship, offering a solid foundation for both parties to thrive.

CONCLUSION

Reflecting on the Journey

As we draw to a close with "Navigating Bipolar Disorder," it's pivotal to reflect upon the intricate journey that unfolds when one grapples with such a multifaceted condition. This guide has sought to illuminate the labyrinthine paths of bipolar disorder, aiming to arm both those directly impacted and their surrounding support systems with knowledge, strategies, and above all, understanding. The journey through the landscape of bipolar disorder is fraught with challenges; yet, it is equally punctuated by profound moments of growth, personal victories, and an ever-present thread of hope that weaves through the narrative, offering solace and direction.

This journey is not solitary. It involves an intricate dance between the individual navigating their bipolar disorder and the constellation of supporters—family, friends, caregivers—each playing a vital role. The essence of this book is to highlight the importance of empathy, open communication, and mutual support. Through shared experiences, victories, and setbacks, a deeper understanding of the disorder emerges, fostering a community that is both resilient and nurturing. The dialogue around bipolar disorder is enriched, moving beyond the realm of medical definitions to encompass the lived experiences of individuals, thus painting a fuller, more human picture of what it means to live with bipolar disorder.

Hope, a central motif, casts a luminous glow on the path forward. It is hoped that anchors us amid the storm, offering glimpses of calm seas ahead. It speaks to the potential for stability, the promise of understanding, and the prospect of a life where bipolar disorder informs but does not define one's existence. This hope is not unfounded; it is built on the solid ground of advances in treatment, the power of supportive relationships, and the resilience that comes from facing and overcoming challenges. It encourages us to envision a future where managing bipolar disorder is integrated seamlessly into the tapestry of life, allowing individuals to pursue their aspirations and lead fulfilling lives.

Empowerment threads through the narrative, underscoring the collaborative effort required to navigate bipolar disorder. It is about building a future together, one where individuals with bipolar disorder and their support networks co-create a framework of care that is holistic, compassionate, and adaptive. This book endeavors to be more than a guide; it seeks to be a companion on this journey, offering insights and reflections that resonate with the experiences of those it seeks to support. It champions the notion that, together, overcoming the challenges of bipolar disorder is not only possible but can also be a source of strength and growth.

In the concluding chapters, a call to action emerges, inviting readers to engage in advocacy and raise awareness about bipolar disorder.

This is about more than seeking better treatments; it's about changing how society views and responds to mental health. It's a rallying cry for inclusivity, understanding, and respect, urging us to advocate for a world where mental health is valued as an integral part of overall well-being.

As we contemplate the path forward, let us carry with us the lessons learned, the strength garnered, and the love shared throughout the pages of this book. "Navigating Bipolar Disorder" is a testament to the journey of understanding, managing, and living with bipolar disorder. It's a narrative that intertwines the challenges with the triumphs, the setbacks with the steps forward, all the while guided by the beacon of hope. As we look to the future, let us do so with the conviction that, through empathy, knowledge, and united effort, navigating bipolar disorder is not only a path to managing a condition but also a journey toward understanding the depths of the human experience.

9 798321 250983